DANG NEAR
Royal

A Dramatic Comedy

by

MILAN SERGENT

Reviews for
Dang Near Royal

"Dang Near Royal by Milan Sergent had me in stitches . . . . This is the deep south meeting stuck-up toffee-nosed Britain and it is comedy at its finest. We get to know the amazing, colorful characters very well and some of them you will really get to know – you'll soon know whose side you are on! . . . This is all go right from the first page, a truly down-to-earth comedy with a touch of the bittersweet to it. Milan has written a story that you can only truly appreciate if you understand British humor. I do and I think this would go down a treat as a made-for-TV series in the UK."

—Anne-Marie Reynolds for *Readers' Favorite*

"Dang Near Royal by Milan Sergent is one of the best comedy novels I have read for a long time. I found the clever play on words and the results of miscommunication throughout the plot absolutely hysterical. The characters each had unique personality traits which made for some incredibly humorous interactions. . . . The comedy was consistently witty and sharp. This novel, however, is far more than a continuous stream of slapstick and hilarious situations; there are also wonderful relationship developments, and the bonds between the members of the Gurney family were completely endearing. The ending was a really good example of the importance of trusting your basic instinct when it comes to evaluating the goodness in people. I highly recommend this novel to anyone who loves well-thought-out and intelligent humour."

—Lesley Jones for *Readers' Favorite*

"Dang Near Royal is a satirical dramedy written by Milan Sergent. . . . Funny, clever, and at times surprisingly poignant, Dang Near Royal is delightfully outrageous. Milan Sergent's novel is tightly-paced and provides ample entertainment from start to finish. I gobbled it up in one sitting and just couldn't put it down. The characters are quirky and colorful, and despite their inherent flaws, you can't help but root for them. . . . In his quest for humor, author Milan Sergent pulls no punches and makes fun of both southern stereotypes and English aristocracy in equal measure. Dang Near Royal is an absolute riot that I would readily recommend to anybody itching for a hysterically funny read."

—Pikasho Deka for *Readers' Favorite*

". . . This is a dark comedy that boldly addresses the unthinkable. In an age where many of us are weaned on mindless reality TV programs, Dang Near Royal reminds us that our gullibility can lead to our downfall. I am impressed by Sergent's daring and frank illustration of the exploitative world of reality television. He gives you a thorough look at how the minds of his characters work in a plot that operates like a sitcom. Perhaps the hidden message in Dang Near Royal is that reality television is nowhere close to simulating reality and that it is even getting worse at representing the real world. This novel becomes a must-read, because its balanced drama and humor are relevant, and you want to find out if the Gurneys will emerge from that veil of superficiality."

—Vincent Dublado for *Readers' Favorite*

"As a first-time reader of Milan Sergent, I certainly was not disappointed. Dang Near Royal is a laugh-out-loud book with elements of realism about the everyday concept we have of the lower side of aristocracy, always making more of themselves than is absolutely necessary. Milan Sergent brings the characters to life with all their foibles, making you have a real feeling of love or loathing for each one. He goes to great lengths to bring what would otherwise be an outrageous story into the realm of humor and succeeds wholeheartedly in making you laugh and cry with frustration at people's antics.... A wonderfully written, funny, and sad book that will make your heart rejoice in the end!"

—Bernadette Diane Anderson for *Readers' Favorite*

Thank you to Barbara B., Christine, Melinda,
Stacey, and Stella. Your insight was invaluable.

To my beautiful and talented wife, Author Beatrice H. Crew.
Thank you for your years of devotion.

Published by Cryptic Quill Publishing LLC.

ISBN 13: 978-1-954430-02-0

Library of Congress Control Number: 2021907340

TABLE OF CONTENTS

CHAPTER ONE 1

CHAPTER TWO 12

CHAPTER THREE.. 22

CHAPTER FOUR.. 29

CHAPTER FIVE 54

CHAPTER SIX.. 74

CHAPTER SEVEN 87

CHAPTER EIGHT 96

CHAPTER NINE.. 104

CHAPTER TEN... 128

CHAPTER ELEVEN... 144

CHAPTER TWELVE... 153

CHAPTER THIRTEEN... 162

CHAPTER FOURTEEN.. 183

ABOUT THE AUTHOR.. 190

Also Available by Milan Sergent.. 191

CHAPTER ONE

Derick put his phone on speaker. He could barely hear it dialing his ex-assistant over the noise of the protests out on the street. This was finally it. He held the sharp edge of a letter opener across his left wrist, just below his gold and diamond watch.

Someone answered.

"Don't even ask where my safe location is, Derick Hosier. I'm watching the news right now. It's really awful," shouted Suki. "Regret firing me, do you? Well, you can't toss me aside and still expect me to get you out of every situation."

Derick tiptoed over to his office window and peeped through the blinds. He listened for the fire alarms. From either gunshots or firecrackers, he wasn't sure, but smoke was now rising to the third-floor window. He couldn't even see the lushly landscaped yard in front of his office building or the broad street beyond that. For nearly a mile in front of his prime block of Los Angeles real estate, people stood elbow to elbow, yelling and holding up signs with various messages: Stop Human Trafficking! – End Slave Labor! – And the worst signs of them all: Kill the

Pedophiles!

"Suki! Listen, Suki, this mob is going to kill me. I've been trapped in my office for three solid days. You've got to do something, or I swear to the media gods I'm going to end it right here."

"Gotta go. Someone is banging on the door," said Suki, with a tone of panic Derick had never heard in her voice before.

Derick couldn't believe the events of the past few months had come to this. He thought back to the beginning, hoping to come up with a believable defense— if he survived to get his day in court.

Two Months Earlier

April 2, 2019

Hosier Pictures

Los Angeles, California

3:47 P.M.

The phone wouldn't stop ringing. Closing his laptop, Derick rubbed his aching eyes. He hated social media sites more than anything; a bunch of unruly nobodies, pretending they like everyone they ignore in their friend lists—always trying to impress strangers. His job was getting people to do what he wanted, speak how he wanted, wear anything or nothing if he wanted. He could tell by the incessant but distant tone of the ring it was

Millie S. Pimbledon. If he picked up the receiver, his headache would only get worse. If he didn't pick up the receiver, he might not get paid for the year.

"Derick Hosier."

"This is Lady Pimbledon. It's nearly midnight here in Northamptonshire. I've tried to reach you all day. Is this how someone with royal blood is treated in your country? This is dreadfully unfair. I don't have much time left; you know. What happened to that, that gal working for you?"

"You mean Suki?"

Derick cupped his hand over the receiver when Suki finally strutted into his office, embracing her hot-pink designer briefcase as though it held the Holy Grail. With red veins popping up in her eyes, she shook her head, signaling to him that she didn't want to talk to Millie.

"Suki is, uh, out of the office today. She is certain she has found your last of kin," said Derick.

"Oh, do tell me they aren't Americans. No offense, but you know how I detest most of you Yanks. I'm sixtieth something in line to the throne, you know."

"Um, no—no, I'm certain they aren't Americans, Lady Pimbledon," said Derick, holding the phone farther from his throbbing ear and returning Suki's petrified gaze.

"Well, they're not new money, I hope," said Millie. "You know how I feel about people who work for money instead of just having it; they're so desperate. I was once the crème de la crème of British society, you know. I can't have the carefully bred ruling class thinking any less of my—"

"Hold on," said Derick, clicking a button on the phone. "I think it's Suki on the other line now. I'll call you back as soon as I get the latest update. Good afternoon—uh, I mean good morning."

Derick hung up the phone. His eyes sagged at Suki as he held the letter opener against his wrist.

"I'm the only film producer in L.A. about to lose everything if we don't get a hit reality show soon. People are starting to question, you know, what sort of business we're actually operating here."

"On with that load of tosh again, are we, Derick?" With a smile that encompassed her three shades of pink lipstick, Suki grabbed the letter opener out of his hand. She placed her briefcase on the desk and removed a file folder from the top of a messy stack of papers. "I've searched the Library of Congress, every social media account, and every genealogical research site—"

"You found something!" Derick grabbed the file folder, but Suki gripped her end in a tug of war.

"Now, it's not conclusive, but I think I might have found Millie's last of kin," said Suki.

"It'll have to do; old Mille's liver won't hold out forever."

"Don't tell me you're harvesting organs now," said Suki.

"At this time, I'd sell your brain if you had one," said Derick. He ripped the folder from her fist and began scouring the photocopied records. He wasn't going to let the finder's reward slip through his hands. It had been a long and exhausting trip to the U.K. to find the right person for his reality show scheme. He needed someone wealthy but out of touch, someone desperate. Discovering Millie S. Pimbledon wasn't hard, thanks to Suki being from London and having more international connections than she had bottles of crazy nail polish. Derick pictured Millie as the perfect "Grande Dame Guignol"—a puppet—like the aging actresses in the 1960s and 70s who resorted to hagsploitation and psycho biddy films to stay relevant. And like many of those aging actresses were promised by their film producers, Derick assured his grande dame that she would be filmed in the best lighting and always from the best angles.

Derick's eyes locked with disbelief when he saw the location of Millie's possible last of kin.

"Of all the places on this enormous and glorious planet the heirs could be hiding, and they settled in Wadebridge, fucking Mississippi!" Derick tossed the folder on his desk and rubbed his chemically frozen forehead. "Give me back my letter opener, Suki. Gimmie—"

"I've only been in this country two years. What is so bad about Mississippi?" Suki asked, keeping the letter opener behind her back.

"For starters, Suki, people with your skin color were once either slaves or hanged from trees there during church socials."

"Don't start pretending you care about people. That's how you make most of your profits—forced labor." Suki slipped the letter opener in the pocket of Derick's suit jacket and patted his left cheek.

"Yeah, yeah. But only recently has Mississippi decided it might be a good idea to remove the Confederate symbol from their state flag—by a contentious public vote, nonetheless."

"Working for you has been a reality horror show. I'm sure I can survive anything," said Suki. "Ah, there's something else about this place you're not telling me. I know you."

"You know the type of heirs Millie is expecting us to just pull out of a hat. I have a feeling you're going to have to work your best magic, or you'll be earning your keep in a snuff film," said Derick.

Suki slinked across the office and fluffed her sherbet-orange afro. "You're not going to be killing me, Derick Hosier—not for one of your D list films. Besides, the old toff shouldn't be too difficult."

"Speak English, Suki, for God's sake," said Derick, stroking his chin.

"I was. Toff is a British term for a wealthy aristocrat like Millie. You convinced her the show's exposure would make her even more money and up her standing in society. Of course, I don't know why she'd need that if she's soon six feet under."

Women like Suki both fascinated and frightened Derick. Surely, most men were intimidated by this rise of women in the business world, no matter how unscrupulous the business. Derick feared the word "phony" was written all over him. Suki could do his job and look ready for the covers of every fashion magazine in the same amount of time it took him to brush the morning coffee stains off his teeth.

"One can never have enough money or fame, dear Suki. Now, book us on the next flight you can. We're going to Mississippi, and you're going to get me those heirs."

"I'll bring the chloroform and an extra roll of duct tape just in case," Suki said with a smirk.

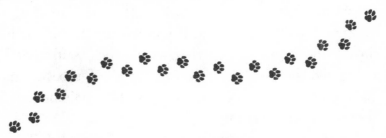

"For God's sake, Suki! Where. Are. You. Taking us?" asked Derick, bouncing from the continuous potholes and popping gravel under the black limo they had rented. He would suggest they head back the way they came, but they had left the Memphis International Airport far behind. For long stretches of road, they passed two deer and dog carcasses, a flattened copperhead, and something that resembled a raccoon. But the dead skunk stench upon entering Mississippi remained trapped in the car for most of the way.

"Haven't got a clue. The GPS keeps leading us in circles," said Suki, steering the car farther down the backroads this time. She tried every station on the radio. "Wherever we are, they only listen to country, gospel, or rap." She paused the tuning button on another preacher giving a sermon:

"My friends, haaa," continued the preacher, sounding like a rabid old bulldog trying to reach a mouse in a hole, "Satan is like a deadly pandemic, haaa. You can't always see him, but he's out there, hiding, sneaking around every corner, haaa—ready to rape, kill, and destroy. He's on the rock and roll radio, haaa; he's in your bedrooms. . . . Friends, SATAN IS IN YOUR CAR!"

"Well, there you go, Suki. That explains what happened to the GPS. And if you ask me, Satan has his cloven hooves on the steering wheel, too," said Derick, acting like he was chewing on a wad of tobacco and making goofy eyes. "No one can possibly be living here." He turned off the radio.

"Look at all the trash on the sides of the road. There must be people living here," said Suki. She passed a discarded sofa overgrown with ivy and looked at the digital map on the dashboard. "According to the map, we're in Wadebridge, Mississippi. And according to the records, the Gurney family are supposed to live somewhere in this abandoned early settlement."

"Perfect!" said Derick, after a moment of silence.

"Who the bloody hell are you, and what have you done with Derick?" asked Suki. She tapped the brakes and searched the roadside trees as if expecting to see bodies hanging from the massive pine limbs.

"I mean—in case the Gurneys aren't really Millie's last of kin—nobody can easily trace them way down here in the Deep South."

"You mean 'the sticks'—speak English, Derick. I just thought of something brilliant," continued Suki, turning on the windshield wipers to knock off the spring pollen and squished bugs. "There is a Wadebridge in north Cornwall, England. All we have to do is claim the Gurneys are from Wadebridge. Millie won't cause a kerfuffle, and you—Mr. hit-reality-show producer—won't be lying—for once."

"That is brilliant, Suki. I might consider paying you someday."

After following the GPS, which told them to make another turn in the road, Suki stopped the car and peered over the jewel-studded top of her designer shades. There wasn't a street sign in sight. If it weren't for two thin tracks disappearing into the tall brush of what once must have been a dirt road, Derick would insist that Suki had lost control of the car and had driven into a forest.

Derick put his wine glass in its temperature-regulated holder. "I don't know if the limo can squeeze through these sticks. I'm afraid we'll have to get out and walk from here."

"Are you daft, Derick Hosier? I'm not stepping one designer shoe out of this car. We've passed at least a dozen Confederate flags and two 'Trespassers Will Be Lynched' signs."

"The last one was a 'Trees-Passers Will Be Lunched' sign," said Derick. "You can't take their threats seriously unless they spell them correctly."

"Are you off your trolley? That's the ones you should really worry about," said Suki.

She lifted her right eyebrow at him and pressed the gas pedal, forcing the limo through the brush, which scraped against the sides of the polished black metal, making Derick's teeth and wallet rattle. He could just see the bill for the damage this trip would cost him.

Within seconds, the dirt trail opened to something close to a dirt yard. Suki reset the car door locks, just in case. Derick couldn't take a breath as his sunshades slid down his nose. He had never seen anything this neglected, even in the last post-apocalyptic movie he had co-produced. To say "standing" was a lie: leaning before them was a crumbling asbestos-shingled farmhouse with several broken-down trucks parked around the small property littered with hubcaps and other debris.

"Go knock on the door," said Derick, while a hound dog with protruding ribs patrolled the limo, barking furiously.

"I'm not getting out of this car, Derick Hosier. Do you even see a front door? I have a skinny neck."

Upon further inspection of the property, they both noticed that the porch roof had collapsed against the railing, leaving a tunnel to access what had to be the front door.

"Tell me this family doesn't use that toilet bowl in the middle of the yard," said Suki.

"Nah, there're weeds growing out of it. I think they intended for it to be a flowerpot at some point."

"They're probably some hippies. Maybe that's how they wipe their arses," said Suki. "And what is that godawful thing sticking out of the ground with all those milk cartons. Is that some sort of voodoo hex?"

"It's what Southerners call a bottle tree—a type of yard art, I believe. They usually hang colorful glass bottles on each tree limb."

Suki angled her head up as she peered out the window. "And I suppose you're going to say that broken doll hanging from that pine limb is art as well—it's a Black doll, Derick Hosier."

Derick leaned across the steering wheel and looked up at the doll in question. He lost his breath, dreading the resistance he knew Suki would give him now.

"Don't ask, Suki. I know what you're thinking."

She rubbed her neck. "These people just can't help hanging something on a tree. It's a warning. We need to get back to L.A." Suki tried to reverse the car, but the tire got stuck in a dirt hole. "Great! We're trapped here—surrounded by that barking beast."

"Honk the horn. Maybe the Gurneys don't know they have visitors."

Suki pressed the horn for ten solid seconds. "Even if the Gurneys do live here, Millie will never believe a family living in this dump could ever be her last kin."

CHAPTER TWO

Alois Gurney stumbled over magazines featuring guns and naked girls now splattered with mold and roach-wing on the den floor. She squeezed past the poison ivy creeping through cracks in the walls in the hall of their two-bedroom home. Her clogged arteries were about to send her into a massive stroke while her husband lay face down on a stained mattress on the floor, his index finger plugging the hole in a half-empty bottle of whiskey. She could just dump a bucket of fire ants on Levi: Even though he was never certified as an air technician, Levi had a job fixing window-unit air conditioners until everyone started using central air. But his years of betting on cockfights, hanging out in honky-tonks, and a handful of bad investments had left their family penniless, but now she was forced to feel sorry for him. He was just diagnosed with some disease Alois couldn't even pronounce other than by its initials, ALS, a deadly nervous system problem her husband insisted they hide from the children.

Alois often wondered how her life had become so hopeless. She hadn't always been so poor: She came from a middle-income family. Her mother left home when

Alois was twelve to run off with some Egyptian man. Her father begrudgingly raised Alois and her stepbrother, who turned to drugs to cope with losing their mom. Desperate to get out of the house, Alois began dating Levi when she was sixteen. When she ended up pregnant, her father kicked her out of their home. And now she was stuck with her mistakes—her precious mistakes.

"Levi! Get yer lazy ass up," Alois stammered, as sweat poured down the back of her neck. "There're some city slickers out there watchin' us, and they ain't a-leaving. I think they're them socialist workers."

"'Social' workers—'social.' Hell, woman."

"Whatever. You want 'em to take our guns or children away? Get up." She kicked his dirty underwear under the half-opened chest of drawers, wondering where she had stored their King James Bible. That always left a good impression on folks snooping around their business.

Levi bolted up from the mattress, accidentally knocking off a figurine of Robert E. Lee from a plastic table with holes burned in it from forgotten cigarettes. He carefully repositioned the Confederate general figurine on the table and placed his whiskey bottle in a coat pocket hanging from a nail on the wall. Together they tore into the children's room. Their fourteen-year-old son, Presley Ernie Gurney, was lying on a mattress on the floor, listening to country music on his headphones. His five-year-old little sister, Tara-Belle, was sticking her doll's broken arms and legs between Presley's dirty toes, annoying him.

"Kids, some bad people are here. Y'all know the drill," said Alois, while Levi pried up a couple of loose floorboards where they often dropped feed for their chickens under the house.

"Aw, Maw. What if we see that rattlesnake again?" whined Presley. His bare chest vibrated while Tara-Belle shoved her dirty fist in her mouth and looked between the floorboards with uncertainty.

"Some critters probably ate 'im. Now git under there, and I'll fix you a big ol' skillet of taters for lunch," said Alois, shoving Presley and Tara through the narrow rectangular opening in the floor before Levi replaced the wooden planks, concealing their children.

Alois could fry up a lump of wallpaper paste and make it taste good. She had worked as a cook in a high school cafeteria until she had Tara-Belle and couldn't afford a babysitter or trust Levi to watch her. Half the time, her car wouldn't even crank, so she couldn't get to no job. Hell, it was costing her family more than she was making. The only problem with having no money was government nosybodies liked to come around occasionally and get all nitpicky if things weren't "up to standard," as they called it. But Alois and Levi didn't live according to the world's wicked standards. Soon, the P.C. police were gonna make her kids stop calling her and Levi "Maw" and "Paw" and start calling them their sperm and egg donors.

"I'ma get the guns," said Levi, heading to the bedroom. "They'll hafta pry 'em from my cold dead fangers."

"Get the fastest guns, Levi. I ain't gonna keep pulling

the trigger." Alois peeked through the white sheet stapled over the broken window blind. Presley thought it would be funny to cut two eyeholes in her favorite sheet—the sheet she had conceived him on nine months before her wedding.

"They ain't a-leaving, I told ya! We had better git this-here shit done and git 'er done now," yelled Alois. It had to be true; too many of her church friends had been saying the deep-state lizard people were abducting children and drinking their blood. The cold metal of the gun now in her hands was her protection burned from God's finger straight into the U.S. Constitution. The Storm was on, as far as she was concerned.

Levi and Alois jerked open the front door and crawled through the crushed rocking chairs under the collapsed porch awning. When their heads cleared the rusted tin, the morning sun blinded them, but Levi kept his gun aimed at the fancy black car anyway. Alois aimed her gun at the windshield, ready to start shooting.

"Look at their car, Alois. I thank them-there folks are the Feds. *Mmmaahk,*" Levi mumbled as he often did, especially when nervous. "I ain't gonna have no fish-bait eating, libtard Yankees putting the Gurneys in jail. WHAT THE HELL DO Y'ALL WANT?" he yelled at the two intruders in the front seat of the car.

Alois's finger throbbed on the trigger when the strange man rolled down the limo window just enough to keep her dog from jumping at him. Lizards ain't never liked dogs. The woman driving the car clasped her hands over her face and lowered her head—probably praying to Satan, Alois imagined, as her blood boiled to the core of her pure heart.

"I'm Derick Hosier, and this is my assistant, Suki. Are you the Gurney family?" he shouted through the window.

"So what if'n we are?" yelled Levi.

"We've, um, been searching for you—you were very hard to trace." Grinning, the man who called himself Derick held up a file folder with photocopied information on the Gurneys. "You all need to come with us. Your whole life is about to change—"

"Outta the car 'fore I fill it full of lead," growled Levi, passing desperate glances at Alois.

"You ain't fixin' to take my family no place," screeched Alois. Her gun went off and blew out one of the headlights on the limo. A few other bullets lodged in the rusted fire barrel under the clothesline where she lit fires to speed dry her underwear in the winter—the reason Levi called Alois "Smokie" whenever he got to feeling frisky. Her hound dog, Egghead, got so worked up it vomited, right where Derick stepped. With her trembling devil-worshiping hands in the air, Suki stepped out of the vehicle last. The chickens bolted from under the house, clucking wildly.

"*Errmumph*. Both of y'all, inside—now," demanded Levi, keeping the barrel of his gun pressed between Derick's shoulder blades. Suki stepped around the animal holes in the yard, careful not to ruin her pink high heels. She jumped when a furry rodent popped out of one of the holes and scurried past the dog.

"What the hell are you thinking, Levi?" asked Alois, keeping her gun on the strangers. "Don't let them lizard people near our children. Take 'em out right here under the eyes of God."

Alois had never seen such a weirdly swanky couple ever set foot in her town. To her, they looked like some of them Hollywood weirdos who pay big money for rabbit food on silver platters. Alois loved the scents they were wearing to cover up their reptile odors. They probably had acute smelling and could detect the sweat and reused frying lard on Alois, she imagined too easily. Not just for her kids' sake, Alois didn't want the intruders to see the inside of her crumbling house. Her mind raced at the mess they would find and use against her. She didn't have no fancy house servant, no walk-in closets, and no air purifiers built into the walls.

"Show me your tongues. Stick 'em out," said Alois, hoping to prove to Levi that the intruders were lizard humanoids.

Suki stuck out her tongue and, though it was average-sized, it had a silver earring sticking right through the tip—probably some kind of satanic initiation marking, Alois was certain. She inspected Derick's tongue next. A lump of something green was resting on the tip.

"Ah-ha! Look, Levi," Alois pointed at the man's tongue with her gun. "He eatin' on a marijuana pill."

Derick spat out the pill. "No, that—that was just a breath mint—halitosis." He grinned.

"I don't care what flavor you call it. I know drugs when

I see 'em," said Alois. "I'll bet you wanna come inside our house and have some pizza. Yeah, didn't think I knew all about your Luminati code words, did ya?"

"What in the hell are you talking about? We ain't got no pizza ta offer nobody," said Levi, while Suki and Derick exchanged terrified glances.

"Pizza is the New World Order's code word for pedophile hookups—something to do with triangles and cheese and our Godsent president time traveling," said Alois. "I told you to stop skippin' church, Levi. You'd know all about these thangs. You're either a part of The Storm, or you're gonna be swept up by it."

"A'ight, woman, but we ain't a-shootin' nobody out here," said Levi, looking around nervously.

After he forced the intruders into the den, Levi ordered them to sit on a burlap sofa, where rips and stains and dirty clothes nearly obscured the orange and brown plaid pattern.

"You're making a big mistake. We are not pedophile lizard people," said Suki. She frowned at the empty cigarette packages Levi used for wallpaper.

Alois sneered. "Hell, of course you ain't gonna confess to it! Satan is the Father of Lies and the Lord of the Flies, and I can hear the little wings flapping every time you open them mouths of yours." Alois got a chill when she heard a flapping and tried to distract the intruders from seeing a big fat cockroach crawling on the broken chandelier that Levi had secured above the kitchen sink with a dozen bent nails. The darned roach had to go and cling to the only prism left on the one nice item in her whole house.

Alois took the gun from her husband. "I got this, Levi. You go check on the young'uns under the house."

Suki cringed when everyone heard Levi prying up the floorboards. Alois aimed the gun between the two strangers. "Now," Alois continued, "it might not look like it, but me and my husband ain't bad parents. We just ain't rich and showy like you, that's all."

"No, but you're about to be," said Derick, when Levi returned with Presley and Tara-Belle. The children's eyes grew as wide as chicken eggs when they saw Alois aiming the gun at the strangers.

"That's why we came all the way from Los Angeles," Suki added, with her head turned from the barrel of the gun.

Alois rolled her eyes. "We didn't enter no sweepstakes. Stop blowin' smoke up my—"

"Tell 'em what I told you," Levi whispered to the children.

Presley and little Tara-Belle eased toward the sofa where the strangers sat, terrified. "Please don't take us away from our maw and paw," said Tara-Belle, before sobbing behind her dirty hands. Her face had become so grimy from hiding under the floorboards that her freckles had disappeared. She squirmed in her pink cotton dress.

"We aren't being mistreated or nothin'. We're—we're happy living here," stuttered Presley in his monotone drawl. His bare chest heaved, and his hands fidgeted in the torn pockets of his blue jeans. Bits of chicken feed fell off his dirty stomach.

Suki reached past the gun and placed her hands on Tara-Belle's tiny shoulders. "Aw, sweetie, we're not here to take you away from your parents. These poor babies are upset. Show them your business card," Suki said to Derick.

"Don't you molest *my* children," growled Alois. She pulled her children behind her while Derick removed his engraved business-card holder from his suit coat. Levi snatched it from the man's fingers and pulled out a card.

"You're a film prodder?" asked Levi, after studying the card with a wrinkled forehead.

"A film *producer*. That's right," said Derick, taking back his cardholder with a strained smile. "You are Levi Waylon Gurney, aren't you?"

Levi nodded reluctantly, and Derick scooted to the edge of the sofa. "I've been trying to tell you who we were ever since we arrived. Apparently, you have a great aunt in Northamptonshire, England, who is dying of liver disease."

"What aunt?" asked Levi, jerking his head back with a dimpled chin.

"Her name is Millie S. Pimbledon, and, my good man, she is unbelievably rich." Derick's eyes sparkled wildly, and he eased closer to the edge of the sofa as if desperate to say something else.

"Oh, my husband ain't got no kinfolk who go by no double-barreled name like that. You got the wrong Levi," laughed Alois, lowering the gun.

"We've checked every record in existence. Trust me, your husband is the only Levi Waylon Gurney who's ever lived," said Suki.

"Excuse us for a minute, and don't go a-trying anything funny," said Alois. Her blood seemed to tingle in her veins. She pulled her husband toward the front door under the Confederate cavalry swords crossed overhead— "Calvary" swords, Levi and Presley called them. Alois needed to have a private discussion with her husband but kept her eyes on her children, who remained six feet away.

CHAPTER THREE

Alois clung to the front door but kept looking at Derick and Suki, the strangers who showed up on the Gurney's property, claiming they were about to make her family of four rich. Levi stood close to her. His plaid flannel shirt reeked of smoke and sweat, something Alois had never noticed until she had fancily dressed visitors enter her home for the first time, stirring the musty air with the smell of roses, citrus, and heaven.

"I don't trust those two as far as I can spit a watermelon seed. Do you know what they are talking about? Do you remember your folks taking you to England?" Alois asked her husband.

"Ain't got no clue. My maw died when I was 'bout Presley's age. We never went nowhere. The only vacation we ever took was a long-ass drive to the Arizona desert 'cause Paw just had to see some famous cowboy's grave marker. We looked at the marker, said a prayer, ate mayonnaise sandwiches, and drove back home. Maw hardly ever talked about none of her family—said they was all worldly and needed to git right with Jaysus Christ— made us rememberize that-there scripture 'bout shunning family—what were it? One or Two Corinthians 5:11, I thank."

"Why would yer momma give up who knows what kinda spoiled-rotten life over there in England to live here in poverty instead? Your father wasn't from England, was he?" asked Alois.

"Naw. Paw was as 'Merican as they git," said Levi.

"Didn't you say he was a pastor when he met yer momma?"

"Paw weren't no run-of-the-mill preacher; he was a tongue-talkin', holy-rolling, Pentecostal preacher when I was little. He had us afeared even using the bathroom was a sin."

"I don't understand. He shoulda made a good living then," said Alois.

Levi lowered his head. "He got caught sleeping with the church secretary. Lost everythang, even the shirt off his back. Maw never forgave 'im even to her death."

"Ah, the devil got a hold of yer daddy then! Maybe this Millie woman is your grandmaw's sister, Levi. Maybe she's on the devil's side, too. Reckon your poor momma had no choice but to disown her. Maybe Millie might be needing somebody to unload all her money on after she kills over."

"Now, Alois, you accused our visitors of being devil-worshipin' lizard people. And now you thank it's a'ight to take the devil's money? Just listen to yerself sometimes," said Levi. "You need to calm down with all these crazy science fiction stories you keep spouting off."

Feeling betrayed, Alois scowled at her husband. "Levi Gurney! You mean you don't love Jaysus anymore?"

Levi's stubbly chin wrinkled, and he closed his eyes, which were growing duller each passing day.

"We need to face it; the doctors around these parts have given up on me. I'ma be dead soon, and Jaysus ain't done much for me, now has he? Besides, you almost killed them-there people. If they was here to be touching our kids, they'd be packin' some ammo on them is all I'm sayin'."

"Oh, Levi. What're we gonna do? We've been holding these nice people hostages. I busted up that big ol' fancy car of theirs! Unless they're foolin' us, then we could be facing jail time." Alois held a trembling hand over her sweaty forehead. "But if they ain't tellin' no lies, this might be the only way to keep from losing our kids—if something happens to you. We ain't got no insurance, Levi. We should at least discuss the details with them. Maybe that Millie woman does want to leave us all her money. Just thank: we could pay for them expensive medical treatments like they have in those big cities—treatments you desperately need and—"

"A'ight, I'm fixin' to find out what's what," said Levi, visibly uncomfortable talking about his illness. "But you gotta let me handle this now."

Levi crept up to the sofa and stood with his head down in front of Derick and Suki. He removed his camouflaged baseball cap as an afterthought. "*Errmumph*. I'm afeard we, uh, we didn't get off to a good start this morning—"

"Would, uh, you two like some faucet water?" Alois asked the guests. She plucked two dirty Mason jars from a pile of dishes in the sink. "I can git y'all some—after I wash them, of course."

"No, thank you," said Suki, playing with Tara-Belle, who kept handing her broken limbs from her dolls.

This and the filthy jars in her hands unnerved Alois as if she were suddenly seeing the wretched mess she had made of her and her children's lives: She had to be the worst mother on the planet. And what had ever brought her to the place that she would start shooting guns at innocent people based on her stupid paranoia? Even if one of the strangers had dyed sherbet-orange hair. Alois hadn't been able to color her hair in a year. Her ends were now brassy, and she had long patches of gray and black, which she tried to hide by pinning it all up with dozens of ugly bobby pins. Her children deserved to have a better life, better parents.

"Levi wants to apologize fer getting a little carried away," said Alois. She swept a pile of crumbs and food debris off the kitchen counter onto the wood plank floor, then straightened a crumpled hand towel on the stove handle to hide stains on the oven window. "He thinks he might be related to that Polly Bibbleton woman after all. Don't you, Levi?"

"'Millie S. Pimbledon,'" said Derick, while Levi mumbled and nodded.

"Levi needs to discuss our part in that 'us about to get rich thang' you mentioned—don't you, Levi?" said Alois.

"He wants to know what we're supposed to do to git the money."

Derick jumped up from the sofa, opened the folder he had been holding, and removed a stack of papers. "My man, your life is about to be changed in ways you never thought possible. We're talking millions of dollars. All you and your lovely wife have to do is sign these papers, saying you and your family will agree to star in a reality show called The Benefactrix, the story of Millie S. Pimbledon's last days and her search for her remaining relatives. You see, the poor woman is dying of liver disease and wants to leave Therapon Hall, her estate, and her fortune to her last of kin. And when I say estate, I mean a manor house the size of—what is this town called, Suki?"

"Wadebridge, Mississippi." Suki handed Derick a flashy black pen from her purse.

"I'm telling you, my good man, you aren't going to believe your eyes when you see what's about to be yours." Derick handed the pen to Levi and knocked the potato chip bag, unpaid bills, and empty beer cans off the coffee table, where he then placed the papers. Suki twitched on the sofa as if a bug had crawled down her arm. Alois and her children gathered around, trying to see the writing on the paperwork. Alois was plumb-near sure the words would sparkle; it sounded too good to be true.

Levi couldn't read worth a damn, and Alois knew she'd have to take over so her husband would avoid gittin' all embarrassed. Even she could hardly ever read the tiny print on contracts—all the big words meant to confuse folks. Already Levi was squinting at the contract and rubbing the razor stubble on his leathery chin, pretending he was seeing right through a bucket of hidden catches.

"We need some time to thank this over," said Levi.

Derick placed one arm around Levi. "You could, Mr. Gurney, you could." He looked at his gold watch. "But Millie S. Pimbledon probably won't hold out much longer, and it would be a shame to let a fortune like that just slip through your hands."

Alois snatched the contract from Levi and sped-read the top page. "This ain't gonna cost us nothing, is it? 'Cause we ain't gonna be paying no hidden fees."

"Not. One. Penny, Mrs. Gurney," said Derick.

Levi glanced apologetically at Alois. Then his chin lowered to his children, who clung to his side with the same anticipation they used to get at Christmas before they realized their handful of "practical" gifts were now coming in a brown sack from the dollar store. Levi handed the pen back to Derick.

"*Hmmaarr...* sorry, Mr. Hosier. I don't thank I'm gonna be signing this-here contract. We ain't got no means of going to England. I ain't gonna be filmed looking like a fool."

Presley's bare stomach swelled with a loud sigh. His voice cracked. "But why won't you sign it, Paw? I get made a fool of every day at school."

Suki bolted up from the sofa and knelt in front of Presley as his eyes grew red and moist. She took his hand. "Oh, sweetie. Do the children bully you at school?"

"They wouldn't if he'd give 'em a knuckle sandwich now and then," grunted Levi.

Presley turned his head and remained quiet for a minute. Suki assured him it was okay to tell her. He braced his dirty hands on his buzzed head and a wrinkle formed on his acne-covered forehead.

"I don't want to finish school. The other kids are mean 'cause of us bein' poor and stuff." Presley sighed again and held his head down in shame. Tara-Belle found her own piece of paper and pretended she was signing her name, using her doll's severed arm as a pen. Her copper-red pigtail braids wilted over her mischievous expression.

While Suki continued to comfort Presley, Derick eyed the contract and licked his bottom lip. "Mr. Gurney, all of the expenses will be taken care of. All you have to do is let my crew film you and your fine family until Millie dies, and we all get our cut of the profits."

Alois clutched the contract to her heart. This was their only hope. For once, she wished her husband would get a spittoon's worth of motivation back and do the right thing before he died, if not for her, then for the children.

Levi's lips compressed. "Give me them-there papers, woman. I'm gonna sign every dang one of 'em in blood if'n I gotta!"

CHAPTER FOUR

Derick held the last page of the contract, ready to snatch it as Alois added her signature beside Levi's name. After she was done, Derick took a photo of it with his leather-covered cellphone, and then he punched a lot of buttons before the phone made a *whooshing* sound. He smiled, and his shoulders relaxed. Alois had never owned a cordless phone. The one wall phone she used to own certainly didn't take pictures or make those funny noises. She couldn't believe Derick wanted pictures of their autographs. He must really think they were gonna be big stars, she imagined. Her chest fluttered, but she was too excited to worry about her heart. She'd soon be rich and start eating that expensive organic junk and have a crew of people to get her all young and healthy, except for drinking, now—everyone had them at least one bad habit. But hell! She might at least get carded for the first time in over twenty years.

"Does this mean I won't hafta go back to school?" asked Presley, while Tara-Bell tugged at his ankles.

"Between shoots, our production company will provide all supplementary education," said Derick. He started to pat Presley's dirty hair but retracted his hand. Suki took a tissue from her purse and wiped off the moist dirt around Presley's confused eyes.

"What Derick means is you and your sister will have your own private teachers and won't have to worry about a bunch of mean kids bullying you. We'll make you a star, and every boy and girl on the planet will be bloody jealous of you."

Presley pulled away from Suki. "If we get lotsa money, I don't need school and stuff. I can just be a racecar driver. Paw already learnt me how to drive a tractor. We can fix up all the cars in our yard."

"Now, young man, you still need to receive an education," said Suki.

"Well, a'ight then; I reckon we better start packing. Is it cold in England?" asked Alois. She grabbed a used garbage bag and began picking up clothes scattered throughout the den. From under a faded Lynyrd Skynyrd t-shirt, a mouse went scampering toward the hall while a few tiny mice droppings hit the floor like black rice.

Suki rolled her eyes toward Derick mighty funny like, Alois thought, as though Suki was dreading him telling her family some bad news. Or did Suki see the mouse?

"I was gonna wash the clothes first, of course. I ain't no pig," said Alois. She lowered the garbage bag on a spot of vomit dried into the threadbare rug.

"There's, uh, one thing we frankly must tell you," said Derick. "You see, Millie S. Pimbledon has, em—what does she call them, Suki?"

"'Issues,'" said Suki, with a regretful frown.

Alois had never heard that word pronounced so endearingly before—kinda sounded like a little doe-eyed girl lisping. What with Suki's fancy accent and all, how bad could the "issues" be? Of course, where Alois lived, folks only had problems—especially with men who speak with lisps.

"You see, Millie S. Pimbledon has issues with the, um, lower-class—especially Americans," continued Derick, while Suki took a deep breath, popped a pill under her tongue, and began rubbing lotion on her hands and elbows. "That's where my British assistant, Suki, here is going to take over."

Suki's eyebrows rose to her orange hair and her lips compressed to a thin horizontal line.

"Take over? Whaddaya mean 'take over'?" asked Alois. She had never had a Black woman take over nothing when it came to her family and such. Especially no gal with punk-colored hair and pink shoes so high she could crack open a watermelon with one step. Already Suki was trying to steal her young'uns over to her liberal ways—make 'em think their maw was a failure. Alois's preacher, Pastor Reverend Deacon Swilley, had warned everyone about folks like Suki and them big city colleges, too.

"That's right. Dear Suki here is going to serve as your speech, etiquette, and fashion coach. She'll have you all passing for posh English aristocrats in no time." Derick looked at his watch as if to avoid the icy glare Suki shot him. "After she takes all your measurements, I'm going to drive back to Memphis and buy you all some proper clothes. You will have to make a good impression on Millie to receive that inheritance."

"*Ermphht*. You didn't say nothing 'bout changing our talkin' and such," said Levi. "This ain't gonna work. I ain't a-doing no show. You ain't makin' no fool of this-here family. Gimme them papers. I'm fixing to tear 'em up!" He dove on top of Derick and grabbed the file folder he had tucked inside his coat lapel.

"But Paw! You can't," gasped Presley, breathing hard.

"Ya get what ya get, boy, and ya don't pitch a fit," said Levi, pointing the folder at Presley before he ran to his room and slammed the door. Alois cringed when she heard her son's distant sobs. Tara-Belle stumbled twice over the floor clutter to check on her brother.

Derick knocked the dust off his coat lapel. "Go ahead and rip up your future, Mr. Gurney. I've already forwarded a copy of the entire contract to my office." He held up his cellphone. "The rules and requirements, in their entirety, were in that binding contract you willingly signed. I gave you and your . . . lovely wife ample time to read it."

"Look," continued Derick as Levi prepared to rip the papers. "I don't want us to have to go the legal route and all, especially after you and Alois assaulted us and held us prisoners. The damage Alois inflicted to the limo headlight will cost more than your entire property. And I can't imagine the compensation for the personal trauma we've endured."

"Oh, Derick, there's no need for all of that," said Suki. "Mr. and Mrs. Gurney, we truly have your best interest in mind, I promise you. All of this pretend will just be until the show is over. Then you can wear and speak whatever and however you want—only you won't have to worry about hiding your children under the floorboards ever again—unless you keep pointing weapons at people."

"You leave my kids out of this." Alois stabbed her finger in Suki's face. "You're all fake. Fake hair, plastic skin, fake tits, and smiles." She closed her mouth, hoping they didn't notice her rotting and missing teeth.

"Look, Mr. and Mrs. Gurney," Derick said with a gentle tone of frustration, gesturing with his hands. "Do you think reality shows are actually reality? No. The people in them put on their best clothes, their best faces, and try to make the television audience think they're something they aren't. But they get rich doing it." He stood up and motioned for Suki to do the same. "But if you want to back out of the contract, I can't force you." They stepped carefully toward the door, and Alois began to panic.

"Give us just a minute," Alois said to Derick, while pulling Levi closer to her.

"We ain't doin' no show. I ain't discussin' it, woman," growled Levi.

"Now listen here," whispered Alois, stabbing her finger in his chest. "You saw your son pleading for a better life back there. We owe it to him, especially after you botched him up with that home circumcision—always trying to cut corners—well, you cut a corner all right!"

"Hush your mouth. The boy don't know he's a little different." Levi's jaws clenched, and he cut his eyes around the room, looking to see if anyone had overheard them.

"Presley wouldn't be different if you hadn't of been drinking after I had to home birth him. If—if you had gotten a real job, we could go to the doctors and hospitals like normal people." Alois glared at Levi, hoping he would change his mind.

With a sigh, Levi turned toward Derick and Suki. "A'ight, I reckon we'll be doin' the show and all," he said. "Start measuring us for some new duds. But I ain't making no promises. And you ain't gonna be measuring the Gurney men's thingamajigs." He pointed to his crotch.

Suki's hands trembled as she took a measuring tape out of her purse and began taking the Gurney family's measurements. "To pass off as English aristocracy, you need to stand as tall as possible and act like you are walking on air imported from Buckingham Palace."

"Nah, now," grunted Levi, turning his back to Suki. "I ain't doing none of that light in the loafers, prancin' around mess."

When Suki finally managed to gather Levi's measurements, he left with Derick to the dirt yard to get the limo tire unstuck from the hole. After Suki recorded the others' measurements, she began giving them a crash course on how to talk, walk, and even eat, along with a crash course on British history.

"British history is too hard," sighed Presley. "I can't

remember one George from the other. Did their parents not know what else to call 'em?"

"Whatever you do, keep your teeth clenched when talking and never pronounce the letter R in George or any word. If you don't know the answer to a question, just act snooty and ignore the asker. Also, you want to fraffly people as much as possible."

"What's a fraffly?" asked Alois, practicing holding an invisible teacup. "Is that some word for a wedgie y'all say over there in Britain?"

"Not bloody likely," laughed Suki. "It's the way English upper class say 'frightfully,' only they say it all the time."

"What're they afraid of?" asked Presley, with his chin lifted so high he looked like he had neck trouble.

"Showing their true feelings," laughed Suki. She spelled out the word *frightfully* in the dirt and dust on the floor. "Fraffly means 'extremely' in England. And I'm fraffly sorry to inform you that you must never speak to Millie S. Pimbledon unless she speaks to you first, especially on Sundays. Millie is very devout in her faith, and after church, spends the rest of the day in prayerful meditation."

"Oh, well, that part ain't no problem," said Alois, flinging her hands toward the ceiling. "I loves me some sweet baby Jaysus."

Suki grabbed a scratched-up leather belt off the floor and began to wrap it around Alois's wrists.

"What the fuck do you thank yer doing?" yelled Alois.

She snatched her hands free and raised her fist, ready to punch Suki back to California or England or wherever the hell she was from. "Don't you even think about trying anything with me and my family, you filthy nig—"

"MRS. GURNEY, now, I am trying to do my job here. I know full well what you are capable of doing to Black women such as myself. I saw the doll hanging in your trees."

"Oh, that ol' thang," huffed Alois. "Tara-Belle put that doll up there. She's always climbing trees—anything she can git her hands on. So, if you are calling me a racist, you're dead wrong!" Alois couldn't believe the nerve of a gal like Suki confronting her about anything the way she just did.

Suki stared at Alois with a blank expression. "Mrs. Gurney, if we are going to make you look aristocratic, you have got to stop talking with your hands. You look like you're swatting at flies all the time. This is a technique to train you to keep your arms down." After Alois's nostrils stopped flaring, Suki gently tied the belt around Alois's hands.

"If you're going to get angry, you might consider not talking, period," said Suki, with one raised eyebrow. "If you must speak, never use the words 'ain't, fixin', y'all, or maw and paw' in England, even if your lives depend on it. Never ever shout or act excited about anything. Always keep a stiff upper lip, understand?" asked Suki.

"Yeah, I got it. You want us Gurneys to be like those store mannequins," said Alois. "Nice ta look at but nothing up here." Alois tapped her head with a knowing snarl.

Suki bit her lip and studied Alois with narrowed eyelids.

Alois was getting a headache from trying to remember all that she was learning. She still didn't trust Suki binding her hands. Presley seemed ashamed to even look at his mother now. Alois never thought she would see her son acting this way. How dare he try to make his mother look bad? She wished she could afford to send her kids to private school; those public schools with all that diversity shit were warping decent young'uns like Presley with their so-called political correctness and liberal ways—takin' Jaysus plumb outta schools, her pastor says.

"Ears," Suki said scoldingly. "The English upper class pronounces 'yes' like the word 'ears,' only remember to soften the R." Her scornful gaze paused near Alois's upper chest. "And what is this on your necklace?"

"It's a cross representing our Lord and Savior. It's been handed down through my family," said Alois, wondering why Suki's fingers didn't burst into flames when she lifted the silver chain to inspect it.

"A cross made out of bullets?" Suki rolled her eyes, releasing the necklace. "Mrs. Gurney, you cannot wear that—that thing—in England."

"Now you listen here! This cross ain't ever coming off my neck. That's just what you people would like me to do, ain't it—deny my faith?" huffed Alois. Her wrists tugged against the leather binding.

"Get a real cross—a life-sized cross if you must—and put those bullets back in the Civil War musket you fished them out of," said Suki, folding her arms defiantly. "No woman of class walks around England with artillery missiles around her neck."

After what seemed like a half-hour of Suki and Alois engaging in a staring contest, Presley and Tara-Belle began to look nervous, and so they practiced sipping their invisible teacups. They had drawn in their upper lips so tightly they looked like they were trying to sip tea through their nostrils.

Derick crawled back inside the crumbling house and took the list of everyone's measurements from Suki along with a shopping list she recommended for the Gurneys.

"Remember, Derick, only buy round-toed shoes and nothing in brown. No creased hankies. Get hats and button suspenders for the men. No trousers for the girls."

"Hankies?" asked Presley, nearly popping a pimple on his forehead after his eyebrows rose.

"In your jacket pocket. And you and your father won't take off those jackets until you crawl into your beds at night," said Suki.

Derick paused in the doorway, double-checking the list. "I'm leaving for Memphis now," he said to the Gurney family. "Remember, you must keep everything about the reality show confidential—no talking about any of this to anyone."

"Bless yer little heart. You ain't gotta go all the way up to Memphis. There's a Peggy-Lou's Dress Shack down the holler," said Alois, before realizing she was supposed to stop yelling and soften her Rs, and especially not add them in words like *hollow*. She stood taller, clasped her bound hands together below her waist, and repeated through clenched teeth, "I'm fraffly sorry. Thaez a Peggy-Lou's Dress Shack down the hah-la."

Derick's face screwed up, and he fumbled for the doorknob. "I, uh, I'm pretty certain Memphis will have to do. I'll be back sometime on Sunday."

"What? Y-you're leaving me here . . . overnight?" Suki stammered with bulging eyes.

"It'll give you time to prepare the Gurneys. We have to fly to England in two more days."

Alois felt wheezy in her chest. What if Derick was lying about the reality show inheritance plans and was secretly going to the authorities to have the Gurneys arrested for child neglect and a list of other lies. She started to block the door but didn't want to look suspicious in front of them. Alois had to stop being so paranoid and start trusting people.

After Derick shut the door, Suki took out her portable computer and started typing—probably codes to the home office, Alois imagined, instructing the Feds on how to locate the Gurneys—drop a bomb maybe.

"Mrs. Gurney?"

Alois jumped and started to reach for the kitchen knife Levi had left on the den table to scrape dirt from under his fingernails. She had to get the belt off her wrists.

"Are you okay? You zoned out on me for a minute,"

said Suki. "We need to work on our upper received pronunciation or RP for short. We'll start with you. Your family simply must stop stressing all those 'R' sounds when you speak. To pass as English aristocrats, you can't sound like a bunch of pirates growling all the time. That said, we're going to start with the long single vowel monophthongs. I created a few sentences that I think you'll easily remember."

Suki turned her portable computer around, and on the white screen was the sentence: **The farmer's car was parked far from the barn, and the parts were waiting to be taken apart and recast as works of yard art.**

"We are going for more of a soft 'ah' sound and not an Arrrrrgh! Like this: The fahmus cah was pahked fah from the bahn and the pahts were waiting to be taken apaht and recahst as works of yahd aht."

Alois went first, then Levi, Presley, and lastly Tara-Belle, who got a few of the words right. Presley was able to do the accent the best, and Alois was sure it was because Presley loved cars.

"You have to talk faster and crisper," said Suki. "You all sound as though you've been scrubbing tin roofs throughout a summer heatwave."

By nighttime, Suki removed the belt from Alois's wrists. They had practiced long and short vowel sounds, the schwa, stressed and unstressed syllables, diphthongs and triphthongs, the liquid U, and lastly, the pure T.

"Stop pronouncing Ds in words like butter, letter, Betty, or better. It's not Beddie licked the Budder," said

Suki. "Now, once more, Presley, let me hear you point your lazy tongue. Remember: crisp consonants . . . more forward in the mannerly mouth. Got it?"

"Yes, ma'am," said Presley. "'Cutie Betty and little Patty burned their booties on the rattling kettle, and now they were pretty bitter and a bit skittish,'" repeated Presley. With a red face, he pranced around the room, lisping his Ts and scratching his bare stomach. "Ha-ha-ha! Ow, I bit my tongue."

Alois wanted to crawl under the floorboards; she had never seen her little man act so . . . ridiculous. Levi turned pale, grunted, and slumped in his chair.

"Presley, you are not taking this seriously," said Suki, closing her eyes with a sigh.

"My throat is terribly sore. I can't do no more of this fancy talkin'," said Alois, as the moonlight beamed through the cracks in the walls. Tara-Belle had fallen asleep on a pile of clothes on the floor.

Suki looked at her watch, and then her eyes made a nervous pass around the den and front door. "Very well, we'll continue our lessons first thing tomorrow, and we'll also learn class-based shibboleths of the British aristocracy."

"Shibbo whats?" asked Alois. She cleared the junk off the sofa so Suki would have a place to sleep for the night.

"Shibboleths are revealing words and phrases that immediately signal to the upper class that people like you and I are outsiders." With a frown, Suki kept knocking the dust and bits of food crumbs off the tattered cushions.

Alois suspected there was a fair share of roach and mice dropping on the sofa, but hell! City slickers just shouldn't be so gosh-darn uppity about everything. Folks need to be exposed to germs and nature if they're ever gonna build an immunity. That's what Levi always said, and he was the head of her family the way their church told it should be. Alois would usually be offended that any dark-skinned person would consider themself equal to Alois or her family. Suki, with her swanky job and looks and her high-and-mighty talking—surely, she was considered by the world to be a much higher class than Alois's family. In Alois's circles, folks might not say so, but they all believed minorities should know their place and not shove their business down everyone's throats. Hell! The first thing Alois learned in Sunday School was that good Christians couldn't be part of the world and all of its wickedness, and they couldn't be unequally yolked or yoked; Alois could never remember the right word.

"What's that noise?" asked Suki, sitting all stiff and tight on the center of the sofa.

"That's ol' Egghead. He gets ta howling whenever he spots a critter in the yard," said Levi. "He helps keep the snakes out, though."

Alois balanced a whiskey bottle on the doorknob leading into her kids' room. If Suki or anyone tried to take her children in the night, it would hopefully crash and alert her.

The following day Alois crawled off the mattress beside Levi. She went into the den and found Suki sitting on the edge of the sofa, looking at her watch. She had bags under her eyes worse than Alois had ever seen on a young gal. "You a'ight?"

"Couldn't sleep. I kept hearing something scurrying about in your kitchen," yawned Suki.

"You're probably just hungry. I ain't got much to serve ya for breakfast, 'cept I can fix ya my heavenly manna," said Alois, opening the rusty refrigerator door.

"Not hungry. Sorry," said Suki. She crinkled her nose like she smelled something funny—probably from snorting some drugs during the night, Alois imagined. That's how all those Hollyweird folks keep from eating.

Alois pulled out a three-day-old pot of boiled rice, dumped half of it on four chipped plates, and sprinkled two tablespoons of sugar on top of the rice.

"Please don't tell me. That's what you call heavenly manna—rice and sugar?" asked Suki. She pulled a mirror from her purse and checked her makeup.

"This here ain't just rice and sugar. Ya know what's wrong with you city folks? You ain't got no faith. Pastor Reverend Deacon Swilley says you're supposed to take what little ya have and offer it to the church, and Jaysus will send down manna from Heaven."

"Are you saying that rice—sorry, that manna just fell from the sky?" asked Suki, puckering her lips in the mirror.

"Git behind me, Satan! Food can change; the Vatican once ruled that rats were fish. See that bowl of sugar yonder?" asked Alois, pointing up to the shelf above the oven. "One day, my kids were hungry for something good at Christmas. That-there bowl of sugar sorta fell off that shelf when I was fixin' us some rice. And we got our blessing right there! We have fish more often, too. Sure you don't want some?" she asked, licking the spoon. "Every time my boy eats this, I swear he doesn't cuss as bad."

After the Gurneys finished their breakfast, Suki spent the rest of the day working on their accents and shibboleths. "If you don't use the right words, Millie S. Pimbledon will know you are N.O.C.D."

"What's that stand for—needy and obscene country dummies?" asked Levi.

"It means 'Not our class, dear,'" continued Suki, cracking a smile on her sleepy face while she held her computer screen for everyone to see. "You will refer to restrooms as the loo or lavatory. It's pudding and not sweets, trousers and not your pants. . . . If you are uncomfortable or don't know how to respond to a question, then it is perfectly common to talk about the weather instead." After several hours of Suki relentlessly coaching them, a car horn honked outside, causing Egghead to bark madly.

"That must be Derick!" said Suki, bolting up from the sofa so fast her computer fell on the floor.

"Ears," said Levi, remembering the pronunciation for "yes." Alois beamed with pride. "I'll go and fetch 'im. He's probably afeared, um, I mean afraid of the dog, poor chap."

"Jolly good idea," said Alois. She frowned when Presley and Tara-Belle laughed so hard at their parents' fancy talking that they snorted like pigs.

A few minutes later, Levi and Derick returned with bags and boxes of clothes and accessories. Alois had never seen such swanky packaging. Not even her wedding dress had been wrapped so well—unless you count a shipper's box once full of dried dates as swanky. Levi and his dead parents would probably think she was being worldly and wicked, but Alois couldn't help but touch the bags with their beaded handles and boxes with gold embossing and hand-tied ribbons; they were too pretty to open. Right away, Alois noticed each box and bag had a tag with the name of individual members of the Gurney family, and this helped Suki and Derick separate the purchases.

"Oh wow! Maw, Paw, we got presents," yelled Presley, until Suki gave him a scolding look, and Presley's face became blank and his mood calm. "Frightfully sorry. Mummy and Daddy, I do believe we have gifts."

After the Gurneys tried on their new clothes, they stood as stiff as brick walls while Suki inspected them. "Ah, splendid, splendid. Except sorry, Mrs. Gurney, we really must do something about your hair. We must get you to the nearest salon immediately."

"You can try, but there's only two beauty parlors anywhere near here, and Alois has been banned from both of 'em," said Levi, inspecting his new tweed coat.

"My checks kept bouncing," admitted Alois, sure her face had turned as red as the devil.

"Well, we'll just have to make a trip to the nearest store and get a box of hair color—medium brown should work," said Suki, pulling Derick toward the door.

"Not too brown," said Alois, with a racing heart. "I'm more of a Jaysus blonde, like all the pictures of our Lord and Savior."

"But I just got here," Derick said to Suki, pulling his arm free. Alois was sure Suki had whispered in Derick's ear about "being narked and starved" before they shut the front door.

"Levi!" Alois choked in his ear. "Did you hear that? What if they are with the narks? What if they're here undercover to arrest us?"

"All I gotta say is they must have some mighty swanky jails in Hollywood—making us dress up and all," said Levi.

Alois laughed inside at her foolishness, and she stopped stretching the fabric around her belly. "You're right. Narked must be some sort of British word for thirsty or somethin'. I know I'm gonna need me a big old beer after all of this."

The Gurneys took turns inspecting their reflections in the small bathroom mirror. In her smocked floral dress and hair bow that matched the ones on her pink shoes, Tara-Bell looked like one of the girlie dolls she had always wanted, instead of the broken, naked, and half-bald dolls she had somehow accumulated from the neighbors' garbage cans.

"I'm pretty," giggled Tara-Belle. Her missing front

tooth came into full view as her smile broadened under her freckled cheeks.

Levi stumbled back from the mirror in his tailed morning coat, matching waistcoat, and striped trousers. He turned his head toward the wall. "Gal, you got so many freckles it looks like an old mule shit on you through some chicken wire."

"Now, Levi!" huffed Alois. She had a sick feeling her husband would deliberately make a fool of his family to ruin any chance they had for a better life. She knew his pride was hurt because he could never afford to buy them nice clothes or anything at this point. But she couldn't say anything, not when she would soon lose him.

"We look like fools, Alois. Ain't nobody gonna believe we're no Aristotles."

"Aristocrats," she reminded him as sweetly as she could. "And they won't if you don't at least put in a little effort for once."

Presley tumbled into the bathroom. "Somebody's knocking on the door!"

"They can't be back this soon. Might be some bad people," said Levi.

"Aw, do we gotta hide under the house?" asked Presley, still walking like a toy soldier in his new suit and top hat.

"You'll ruin your clothes. Maybe Derick and Suki forgot something," panted Alois. "Y'all stay back here, and I'll go see who it is."

Alois adjusted her hair and tried not to trip in her high heels as she made her way to the den. She peeped through the holes in the window sheet and couldn't see a car even though Egghead was barking wildly. How bad could it be? She had resolved to stop being so paranoid. She walked to the door and jerked it open. Her mouth became dry; crammed under the collapsed awning were three grown men and four women—her nosy neighbors. Their faces went from looking like ill prunes to stunned peaches.

"Is, uh, Mrs. Alois Gurney here?" asked Mr. Jacobs.

"You're lookin' at her," said Alois, standing as pretty and proper as she could.

"These are for you. We're sorry about Levi," said Mr. Jacobs, handing Alois a wreath of purple carnations.

"What do you mean? Levi is doing good—stronger than ever," said Alois, taking the wreath. They must've heard of Levi's ALS diagnosis, she realized. But how . . . unless his doctor broke his confidentiality agreement and told them? The men eyed Alois from her new shoes to her new accent.

"Well, uh, we heard a gun go off the other day and a bunch of screaming. Then we saw the limo leave here earlier. You mean there wasn't a funeral? You're all gussied up mighty nice—" said Mr. Jacobs, before his wife elbowed him in the stomach, causing him to bend over.

"Levi was shooting at a snake. And that limo belongs to our guests," said Alois.

"So, you plan to continue living on this-here property?" asked Mrs. Jacobs.

Alois smirked. "Why shouldn't I? You seem frightfully jealous about something, if I do say."

Mrs. Jacobs ripped the wreath out of Alois's hand. "We were trying to be nice, honey, but Lord forgive me, I'm done, ya hear? We've formed a neighborhood committee and have gotten a court order. Give it to her, Tommy." She elbowed her husband again, as Alois's heart threatened to give out.

Mr. Jacobs reached in his coat pocket, removed a folded piece of paper, and handed it to Alois.

"You have one week to vacate this property, or they're going to bulldoze it down," continued Mrs. Jacobs, while the other neighbors sneered victoriously.

"Vacate our home? Why whatever for?" asked Alois.

"This property is an eyesore. It hasn't been up to code in years. Not including back taxes you still haven't paid," said Mrs. Jacobs, raising one eyebrow.

Shaking, Alois clenched her teeth to avoid cussing them for everything they were worth. She had never been so angry and humiliated in all her life.

Against her better reason, Alois knew there was only one thing that could redeem her family and get revenge on her self-righteous neighbors at the same time. She stuffed the eviction notice back in Tommy's coat pocket.

"You can shove that stinkin' notice up your bums, and you can have this property, too," Alois tried to keep up her new accent. "Our limo is returning soon." She softened her voice. "In a couple of days, we'll be moving into our enormous castle in England. Levi has a royal great aunt who is leaving us her entire fortune."

The neighbors exchanged looks of disbelief. Mrs.

Jacobs pursed her lips, and her eyes narrowed into slits.

"Well, honey, trash is still trash no matter how expensive the box you squeeze it into," said Mrs. Jacobs.

Alois nearly swallowed her tongue but remembering the stiff upper lip thing Suki had taught her, she wasn't going to let the neighbors see her the least bit rattled. "It's not just the money. The Gurneys are rather big stars now—have our own television series, in fact."

"You mean your family are actors?" asked another female neighbor, who happened to be her church's secretary.

"Frightfully good actors, if I do say. But we've grown tired of lowering ourselves to the neighborhood standards just to fit in. And we thought you would appreciate all of our efforts." Alois gestured toward the collapsed porch awning. "Now, if you'll excuse me, I have to get out of these old rags." Alois caressed her new high cotton dress with its handmade lace collar. "My personal agent and stylist should be returning soon." Alois slammed the door on their stunned faces. She collapsed against the door with chills of satisfaction and dread. Had she just blown her agreement with Derick to keep the reality show and inheritance confidential?

Derick and Suki returned minutes later with a box of hair dye and a hair-cutting kit.

"We just saw the oddest thing on the road that turns onto your driveway," said Derick. "There must have been two dozen people congregated, and they were all pointing and looking at our car. I didn't think we were going to be able to pass them."

"Oh? They've probably never seen a limo in these parts before. They do like to meet at the gossip fence," said Alois.

"While holding a funeral wreath?" asked Derick.

"Oh, that," said Alois, thinking of a fast excuse. "Well, sometimes the neighbors like to, um, mark the road whenever some poor person gets run over."

"Alois, ain't nothin' been run over in these parts except roadkill," said Levi, frowning at her.

An hour later, after Suki had colored Alois's overgrown locks and had trimmed Levi's hair, someone knocked on the front door.

"Just ignore it," said Alois, wrapping her freshly roller-set hair in a towel.

"It can't be somebody at the wrong address again," said Levi. He had obviously not believed Alois's story she had crafted to cover for what she had done. She didn't want to upset her husband or for Derick to know that she had been blabbing her mouth.

Levi opened the door, and it was the mail carrier this time. The man's eyes searched the cluttered home, and then he bowed as if standing before a king.

"The bills wouldn't fit in the box today?" asked Alois.

"Ain't got no mail for you, Your Highness. What's all this talk I've been hearing—you all are dang near royal and got your own TV show even? My goodness!"

Alois stumbled past her husband before he lost his temper. "We're gravely busy—with out-of-town guests.

Off you go now. Pip-pip!" She pushed the mail carrier out the door and locked it fast.

With Derick's, Suki's, and Levi's eyes glaring at her, Alois sent her young'uns to their room to practice their English accents and then spent the next half hour explaining all that had happened and why she had confessed their business secret. Seeing her husband's defeated expression had gutted Alois. However, she didn't mention Levi's illness, as that would have upset her husband even worse.

"I guess this means the show plans are canceled. We'll bag up all the new clothes; maybe you can take them back for a refund," sighed Alois, swabbing her tears on a dirty kitchen rag.

"That was a gross violation of the contract, Mrs. Gurney," said Derick, pacing the floor. "Unfortunately, at this point, I literally have too much invested in the reality show to call it off. You all need to put every effort into making this endeavor a success, or you'll be homeless, I'm afraid. All we can do is hope that the truth of who you are and where you're from doesn't reach the news media before Millie dies, and we get our shares of her fortune."

Suki pulled a white box from a gift bag she had kept close to her side ever since Derick had returned from Memphis. She handed the box to Alois, who opened it with incredible guilt. Inside the box was a glittering crown. "Here you go; a little something from a movie we produced a while back."

"Oh my! Is this—is this a diamond crown?"

"What people don't know won't hurt your reputation," Suki said to Alois, who finally lifted her head from her hands with a bit of promise. "Every aristocratic lady needs an antique tiara for formal occasions. You will pretend it is a family heirloom because it's taboo to buy your own tiara." She placed the heavy and magnificent thing on top of Alois's hair rollers. "When you arrive in England tomorrow evening, you will be leaving all of this behind. Levi will use the title Levi Gurney I of Wadebridge, and you'll be Lady Gurney. Understand?"

"Ears!" Alois and her husband replied, before Presley and little Tare-Belle came from the hall.

"We're not leaving Egghead behind, are we?" asked Presley.

"I'm afraid there won't be room on the private plane for a dog," said Derick.

"Then I'm not going to England," cried Presley.

"Me either," sobbed Tara-Belle, and together they ran to their room.

CHAPTER FIVE

Alois tiptoed to the restroom and back to her seat, afraid to walk too hard in case the plane fell out of the sky as it hovered over the North Atlantic Ocean. She resumed gripping the armrests until she calmed her breathing. None of her family had ever flown before, so she kept looking back at the passenger seats, checking to see if everyone was still alive. Suki was sitting next to Levi, coaching him with his English accent and everything he would need to know about passing as British. Presley kept his face pressed against the plane window, excited that he finally saw land below. Every five minutes, he pressed his finger on the window and asked, "Is that our castle?" Tara-Belle sat on her heels in a seat next to Egghead, fawning over the foxhound's fancy coat and tie that Suki insisted the family pet wear the whole time in England.

"Does that bloody dog have to howl the whole flight? I can't concentrate on giving my speaking lessons," said Suki, who kept spraying citrus air freshener on Egghead.

"That dog of yours is costing me a fortune," said Derick to the Gurneys, finally showing his head from behind a pile of paperwork, including scripts, agendas, and itineraries. "After we land, you can't call that beast 'Egghead.' Aristocratic family pets have pedigree names, and that beast is going to need quite a title to make up for lack of obedience training. You will refer to your dog as Sir Eggart Ambrosias Chanticleer. Understand?"

"Ears," the Gurneys answered.

"The Brits are usually expected to downplay their achievements, which will, um, work fantastically in your favor. Millie S. Pimbledon is going to try to read you all like a book—ask you a lot of questions to see if you measure up. You will simply reply that you don't like to brag and would rather change the subject or something along those lines. Understand?"

"Ears," the Gurneys responded yet again, although Alois wasn't sure she liked Derick's remark.

"Mummy, Tara-Belle stinks," said Presley.

"Oh, Tara, did you mess your panties?" asked Alois, turning around in her seat again.

"I thought I kept getting a whiff of something dreadful," said Suki.

Alois bolted from her chair and inspected Tara-Belle. Something green was protruding from her left nostril. Alois sniffed her face and got a strong whiff of something rotten.

"Tara-Belle, what have you got in your nose?" Alois tried to pull it out, but her daughter cried and started kicking.

"Eww, gross! It looks like a green worm. What if it's stuck in her brain?" asked Presley.

"Stop scaring your sister. I think it's a butterbean sprout. Tara, did you stick a bean up your nose?"

With tears streaming from her face, Tara-Belle nodded. "Yes. I git hungry sometimes, Mummy. I founded it under the oven and putted it in my nose for later."

Alois felt a hot flash of humiliation come over her. Her poor kids were so hungry they were hoarding dried beans. She avoided eye contact with Suki and Derick.

"We can't meet Lady Pimbledon with nose sprouts," said Suki.

Tara-Belle thrashed about and screamed while Alois tried to fish the sprouting bean out of her daughter's nose.

"Could a fellow get a drink on this plane?" said Levi as carefully as he could.

"Me, too," panted Alois, holding up the extracted bean victoriously, with dusty little shoe prints on her dress. "My muscles are tighter than a wedding ring by its fiftieth anniversary."

"I'm afraid not. We're about to land in Northampton and go through customs. I need you all to be as clear-minded as possible," said Derick.

"And another thing," said Suki. "In England, you must never break or jump queue."

"That ain't no problem. I stopped playing pool when I was about nineteen," said Levi.

Suki exhaled deeply and gave Levi an uncertain look. "'Queue' meaning a waiting line of people. We Brits take that very seriously. Do not break queue no matter if your arm has been cut off and you are bleeding to death!"

Derick opened his laptop computer and turned it so the Gurneys could see. "As soon as we arrive at the estate, the show will officially start. A camera crew will be filming you twenty-four seven. The television version will be edited to include interviews of you all, but the internet live feed will be continuous. This is the promo of the show we have so far."

Surrounded by her eager family, Alois got chills when the computer screen lit up with glorious color and dramatic orchestral music, featuring the harpsichord. It made her feel like the time or two when she was lucky to go to a movie theater. Beautiful photos of Therapon Hall appeared on the screen and some shots of the interior. But the images seemed old, Alois thought, as the narrator began to speak:

"Well over four hundred years ago, Therapon Hall stood as one of the most majestic manor houses in the East Midlands. Opulent, enchanting, built to impress. This was the exclusive world of privilege constructed by one of Great Briton's most prominent families. But now it remains in the possession of Lady Millie S. Pimbledon, last of a lineage of aristocrats—or is she?"

The Gurneys sat wide-eyed as the camera panned through the rusted iron gates with the manor house sprawling widescreen in the distance. Ivy had overtaken much of the exterior stone walls, and weeds were overtaking the formal gardens surrounding the property.

"As you can see, the manor house is in need of repair," said Derick, before the narrator continued speaking:

"In its day, Therapon Hall was maintained by nearly a hundred servants, but several years ago, tragedy struck—unforeseeable events that would alter Lady Pimbledon's world dramatically. Now stricken with a deadly disease and down to three loyal servants, Millie has been on a desperate search for her last of kin and has finally found them. Soon to arrive, will the Gurney Family of Wadebridge, England, renew Millie's spirit and ultimately inherit her estate? Find out right here on The Benefactrix!"

"I probably should have told you, Therapon Hall has been neglected, but it is being renovated during film production," said Derick. "Suki and I feel the renovation will add an additional storyline for viewers to follow."

"It's pert near magnificent—the most beautiful house I ever did see," said Alois, reeling from disbelief at the thought of living in something that huge and beautiful.

Suki grabbed Alois's arm, and her brow ridge warped. "Alois, love, I don't know what 'pert near' means in Mississippi, but don't. Just. Don't."

Alois developed a lump in her throat. She had no idea of what to expect. How would her family manage to convince the world they were something they weren't?

As soon as the Gurneys stepped out of the plane, a gang of people dressed in all black surrounded them and began slapping Levi, Alois, Presley, and Tara-Belle in the face with some type of spongy pads. The scent of wilted flowers and chalk floated around their faces. A man started to spray something on Levi's head, but Levi punched him in the nose, sending the man stumbling backward in the airport terminal.

"Whoa, whoa, Levi. What are you doing? You attacked the hair and makeup team," said Suki, picking up the fallen can of hairspray and helping up the hairstylist.

"I'm done! I'm not going to take this abuse," said the stylist, cradling his face in his hands as blood poured from his nose. "You'll be hearing from my lawyer," he groaned, pointing his finger at Derick, while another assistant escorted the fallen stylist out of the crowded airport. He limped and wailed as if he had been run over by a bus, Alois determined. She didn't blame Levi. Even she thought some gang of devil worshipers was attacking them.

"We only have one hour to get the Gurneys camera ready. Millie S. Pimbledon doesn't like to be kept waiting; it causes her to lose her voice," said a female makeup artist, holding a powder puff.

"I have to hand it to you, Derick and Suki; you found us a feisty bunch this time," said a man in dark shades and a pinstripe suit appearing up beside them. "Here is what we agreed on," he said, handing Derick a briefcase. "You had just better hope they don't give old Millie any trouble."

"It 'twas a mistake," Alois assured Derick and the team. "Please continue. It won't happen again."

Levi stilled himself as trembling hands reached out toward his face to apply concealer, mascara, and lip color to his face. A fog of hairspray enveloped his head while another assistant combed his hair. "Need lots of blemish cover over here—semi-matte number twelve," huffed another male makeup artist, after examining Presley's face.

"Acne spackling for Presley," another assistant said, handing over a tub that looked like pale green putty. A woman lint-brushed Alois in areas she had never been touched by a stranger. Out of nowhere, Tara-Belle broke into loud sobs while Presley spat and wheezed as though he had eaten a mouthful of makeup.

"That girl doesn't ever do as she is told," said Levi.

"She's just tired from the long flight," said Alois.

Suki knelt in front of Tara-Belle, while another assistant burned her finger with a curling iron from Tara-Belle jerking her head. "It's okay, sweetie. You're a little princess now, and little princesses have to be made pretty every day. Derick, I think we should give her that gift now." Suki snapped her fingers and pointed toward the luggage still piling up, thanks to the plane attendant.

Derick groaned, dug through the luggage, and pulled out a rectangular box. Suki took the box and opened the lid in front of Tara-Belle. Her eyes lit up, and her fingers reached for the expensive doll in a pink silk dress and a little sparkly crown nestled over its long blonde ringlets. Another assistant placed Alois's tiara on top of her head and pinned a few loose curls to secure it.

"See, your doll is a princess, too," said Suki. "And every day when the beauty team makes you pretty, you can make your doll pretty, too. Okay?"

"Ears," said Tara-Belle, sniffling one last time. Sir Eggart Ambrosias Chanticleer howled pitifully when one of the makeup artists began applying mascara on his whiskers and eyelashes and a bit of sparkly copper eyeshadow to the brown patches on his hairy face.

One hour later, the driver steered the stretch limo through the gates of Therapon Hall as the sun was beginning to set.

"Drive slowly. We want the home viewers to anticipate the Gurneys' introduction—the grand unveiling," Derick ordered the driver.

Several camera operators lined the sides of the long gravel drive, filming their arrival. One of Millie's servants, a dark-haired boy in his late teens, closed the gates, nearly stumbling as his head remained turned toward the car as it traveled toward the manor house.

"Wow!" said Presley, as he and Tara-Belle climbed over one another to get the best view of the estate. Alois felt as though she had arrived at a sprawling old city instead of a manor house.

"Will you look at that," said Alois, nudging her husband, who sat next to her, rubbing his eyes and looking pasty from the makeup that had covered his sunburned skin. Compared to her house in Mississippi, she imagined, it was a pristine palace.

"What are all those tiny helicopters flying around?" Alois asked.

"They're not helicopters; they're drones—part of the audio and video production," said Suki, airbrushing pink makeup onto her cheeks with a jewel-covered bottle. Alois got a lump in her throat again. The only thing buzzing around the air in Mississippi was disease-carrying mosquitos.

"You'll have to fend for yourselves from this point on. Suki and I will be working behind the scenes," Derick said to Alois and Levi, before squirting something minty-smelling in his mouth.

"Remember," Suki whispered to the Gurneys with her quivering hand tugging the jadestone necklace around her throat, "here you eat with your forks in your left hand, tines down, and you hold your knife in your right hand— as I showed you. Cut everything into tiny pieces, even if they toss you a banana on the bloody cricket field. No big bites."

"I don't know if I can eat food on the back of a fork, but I'll try," said Alois. She imagined the English made dining a balancing act to avoid eating so fast. Gluttony wasn't a sin in her hometown, and Mississippi almost always ranked the highest in fattest states in the country.

Another servant, a man in his early sixties with thin gray hair, big ears, and a bulbous nose, opened the limo door for Levi while a camera and spotlight remained on them. As formal as a soldier in the royal guard, he turned toward the cameras.

"Presenting Lord Levi Gurney the First of Wadebridge," the servant announced. Then he opened the other doors in sequence and announced, "Lady Alois Gurney. Lord Presley Ernie Gurney. Lady Tara-Belle Gurney. And lastly, hem-hem," he said after a visibly stunned pause and checking a notecard in his white-gloved hand, "I present Sir Eggart Ambrosias Chanticleer."

Alois remembered what Suki had told her about not showing excitement: "Look as though it's a sacrifice of your time to enter that common old mansion." But Alois's subtle attempt at snooty inconvenience vanished as fast as dollar-store deodorant in a marriage-equality protest during a Mississippi summer. She wanted to crawl back in the limo when her dog, with its hotty toddy new title, jumped onto the gravel and squatted on its hind legs, leaving a pile of poop, which the teenage servant slipped on while taking the luggage from the driver. Suki and Derick sneaked out of the limo after the cameras spun toward the Gurneys.

"Welcome to Therapon Hall, Your Lordship and Ladyship. My name is Mr. Shaw," said the elder servant before pointing at the other two servants. "This is Ms. Johns, and the young man with excrement on his shoe is Taylan Chowdhury. Lady Pimbledon will grace you with her presence soon in the dining hall. She's rather eager to meet you," he said in a deep, no-nonsense voice.

A female director with a blonde ponytail stood on a wooden box and motioned for the Gurney family and three servants to line up into two groups at the manor house entrance. Alois felt as though her family was standing in front of a firing squad, and the bullets would blow their cover with one pull of a trigger.

"Welcome to the first episode of The Benefactrix, Great Britain's first reality show of death, dynasty, and discovery. And here they are finally arriving; Millie S. Pimbledon's long-awaited last of kin!" said the male host in a pale-yellow suit and green bowtie. "We are moments away from the Gurneys' first meeting with the now elusive Lady Pimbledon. A lot is at stake here. Will Millie approve of her long-lost heirs? Will we learn anything about this mysterious family from Wadebridge, England, or how Therapon Hall fell into the near state of disrepair we see here today? With months—weeks perhaps—to live, Lady Pimbledon has agreed to let viewers inside her secret world of privilege and scandal. Each passing day, the Gurneys will either score or lose points with Millie that could cost them their inheritance. Of course, you, the viewing audience, will get a chance to influence her decision at the end of each episode. Until the nail-biting moment that her last will and testament is read, you will have front-row seats to eavesdrop as upstairs and downstairs occupants of a once-grand manor house cross paths, as master and servants are forced to mingle with nowhere to hide. All right here on The Benefactrix!"

The director rolled his finger at Mr. Shaw for him to go ahead.

"This way to the dining hall," said Mr. Shaw. The Gurneys turned down several halls, and before the servant opened the door, he whispered to Levi and Alois, "It is customary to bow before Millie S. Pimbledon."

Wearing white gloves, Mr. Shaw opened the doors and led them to a magnificent long table covered in silver service and blue and gold china. The fragrant flower arrangement and burning candles on the table sweetened what would surely be years of old wood polish.

"It is customary for dinner guests to stand next to their assigned chairs on opposite sides of the table until Millie arrives," Mr. Shaw told the Gurneys.

Cameras, microphones, spotlights, and silver reflectors remained glued on the Gurneys. The hall was so large and sturdy, even the slightest stomach growl amplified vulgarly. Ten minutes later, a woman in her early eighties shuffled into the dining room. She looked as if someone had stuffed her inside her faded, seafoam-green gown with a white fur collar. A tiara much grander than Alois's stood atop her brassy golden hair. A strange fluttering around the woman's head made Alois imagine she was tired from the long flight. She looked harder and noticed that someone had clipped nearly a dozen live butterflies into her helmet of a hairdo.

Prancing beside the bottom of the woman's ballooning gown was a white poodle with a matching tiara and a haircut sculpted in stacked balls like some of the shrubs in the front garden. Alois made a mental note not to let her hound dog anywhere near the gardener.

"It's Millie!" whispered Alois. "Get ready to bow down."

The Gurneys dropped to their knees and bowed against the floor.

Millie paused and inspected them. Her eyebrows rose over her cat-eye glasses sparkling on her pug nose, and her thin lips snarled. Alois looked up and spotted Suki in the corner of the room, waving her arms in protest for them to get off the floor.

"Stand up—quickly," whispered Alois.

"I can't, Mummy," whispered Presley. "I ripped my britches."

"What in the heavens are you all doing?" asked Millie, while the cameras zoomed in on the family.

"Frightfully sorry," panted Alois, standing to her feet. "We were, um, we were looking for Presley's contact lens."

Millie's poodle growled at Sir Eggart Ambrosias Chanticleer, and he whimpered and buried his snout in the hole in Presley's pants, making him squirm.

"Hmm," Millie snarled and continued walking. Her puffy chin lifted as though she were counting the plaster carvings on the ceiling. After ten floral medallions forward, and six to her right, she had arrived at the head of the table where Mr. Shaw waited to seat her. Her poodle he seated in a highchair with a crystal martini glass on its carved tray. For Sir Eggart, he chucked a plain china plate at his front paws.

Millie rang a silver handbell on the table, and Ms. Johns wheeled a serving cart into the dining hall. Compared to Millie's eyeglasses, hers were simple and as harsh as her unhappy expression. Her gray hair was short with a few dull-brown streaks that pointed to the pale mole on her left jaw. With cracked and calloused hands, Ms. Johns began serving soup, starting with Millie first. Suki had warned the Gurneys to watch Millie and use the same eating utensils that she did. Alois was relieved to get that advice because there must've been a dozen different spoons, forks, and knives beside each plate.

Alois was so hungry she could swallow the soup in one gulp. She watched Millie as discreetly as possible, but she didn't choose a utensil. Instead, Millie stared over her cat-eye glasses with suspicion while nibbling on a piece of bread she broke apart with her fingers.

"Did you lose another lens in your soup, or do you all detest smoked haddock?" asked Millie.

Having no clue what smoked haddock was, Alois thought of a fast excuse. She held her jaws nearly clenched like Suki instructed her and focused on speaking more forward in the mouth.

"Oh, no. The smoked haddock looks delicious. It is impolite to start eating before the host does."

"Hmm," Millie snarled. She took her bowl of soup and placed it on her poodle's serving tray. Alois realized the old woman was determined to catch them choosing the wrong utensils and prove they weren't of her class. From the dark corner of the room, Suki held up a silver spoon, which had a more rounded bowl, and she made a backward scooping motion in the air, unlike the American way of scooping soup toward their mouths.

Millie rang her handbell again, and Ms. Johns ran into the dining room, panting for breath.

"There you are," said Millie to the maid. "Before I forget: We've been craving something different for our next meal. Something that starts with a P, I think— panther or penguin meat, perhaps. But not pufferfish; it always feels like such a chore adding that to our delicate diet."

"Certainly, Your Ladyship. I'll add one of those choices to the next menu," said the maid, wrinkling her forehead before easing out of the room.

After studying the Gurneys' dining habits an uncomfortable length of time, Millie dabbed the corners of her mouth with her napkin. "Levi, do tell me what happened to your mother, Mary. The girl just vanished off the face of the earth after my sister, Eleanor, died," said Millie, erupting like a volcano that had been dormant too long. The butterflies in her hair flapped their wings furiously. "Mary must've been so grief-stricken after my sister's death she went into seclusion—well, that's what I tried to assure myself. I mean, why else would the girl turn her back on her family? But who am I? Just her auntie, who tried to shape her into a presentable young lady after her father died so young—that's who." Millie glared at Levi for five seconds. "Well? Please tell me your mother wasn't the ingrate we all took her to be."

How dare this woman call Levi's mother an ingrate— whatever that word meant, Alois thought. She felt helpless as her husband's eyes locked on her then lowered to his soup bowl. She knew he worried that he would flub his attempt to sound like an English aristocrat, especially when he knew nothing about his extended family. It was probably best he remain quiet.

"Levi doesn't know anything about his mum's past," said Alois.

Millie leaned forward in her chair. "Whatever do you mean? Levi is a descendant of my sister, Elanor Seabrooke, is he not?"

"Ears, of course," said Alois. "It's just—"

"Mrs. Gurney, is your husband incapable of answering for himself?" asked Millie, slamming her wine glass on the table, causing the candles to flicker. Ms. Johns took up the soup bowls and then served everyone baked fish. She seemed to linger in hopes of hearing a response from Levi or Alois.

"I tried asking Mummy about her family 'til the day she passed on," said Levi slowly and carefully.

"Before she passed what on—a chronic case of ungratefulness?" asked Millie, taking a tiny bite of fish on the back of her fork, her right hand firmly on her knife.

"He means before she died," added Alois, realizing "died" was the word Suki was desperately mouthing across the room, one of the shibboleths they were supposed to remember. Alois was more uncomfortable than she had been in her whole life. Her new clothes were itchy, her back ached from sitting so straight on the edge of her seat, and she was afraid her tiara would flop over in her plate at any moment—a plate that probably cost more than her whole property in Mississippi did.

"You mean that ingrate never once mentioned us?" asked Millie.

Levi's silverware shook in his fists and his lips compressed. "All she said was, 'You all were worldly, and we should shun Hell-bound people.'"

Alois wanted to crawl under the table with her hound dog. Why did Levi have to word it that way?

"That little ingrate has some nerve calling us worldly. She vanished as soon as her mother cut her off from her inheritance. My dear sister died from the heartbreak of it all. Mary Seabrooke didn't even come to her mother's funeral," said Millie. She rang her handbell more forcibly this time, and Ms. Johns came running into the dining hall.

"You can collect the plates. My appetite has been spoiled," said Millie.

"But, Your Ladyship," gasped Ms. Johns, "what about the other five courses? I prepared butternut squash, lamb chops with balsamic, and strawberry cheesecake with chocolate toffee drizzle. And of course, my special recipe for—"

"Do with it as you please," said Millie standing up from her chair and grabbing her poodle. "Tell Mr. Shaw I've changed my mind. The Gurneys will take the attic rooms instead. And that—that mutt of theirs will have to stay outside from now on." Millie flapped her napkin at Sir Eggart Ambrosias Chanticleer, which was still licking the plate between his paws.

While the young servant, Taylan Chowdhury, tried to drag the hound dog out of the dining hall, Ms. Johns snatched the salad plate out from under Levi, and he stabbed the tablecloth with his fork instead of his half-eaten fish. When the food vanished from the table, Mr. Shaw led the Gurneys into the main hall for what seemed like a half-mile past dozens of lavish but unoccupied rooms with high ceilings.

"Wow, look!" said Presley, taking a few steps up the grand staircase and looking up as far as he could see. His face quickly became expressionless. "I mean, the steps do go frightfully high. I imagine it will take all night to get to our rooms."

"You won't be using those stairs," said Mr. Shaw. "Right this way." He continued leading the Gurney family to the back of the mansion, where they climbed a much narrower staircase for six floors before finally arriving at the attic hall. The rooms along this hall were much less fussy or massive. "You two will stay in this room, and your children will share the room across the hall. Taylan will bring up your luggage momentarily."

"Thank you. Our rooms are simply divine," said Alois and Levi, after Presley and Tara-Belle bolted into their room and bounced on its two twin beds while smiles lit up their faces.

"Right," muttered Mr. Shaw after a pause. His peculiar smirk faded, and two vertical lines formed between his bushy eyebrows.

Levi shut the door to Alois's and his bedroom, locking out the young cameraman who had been following them. Derick and Suki had instructed the Gurney family to pretend the camera operators and production team were invisible. Still, Alois had never felt so creepy in her life. Here she was in a room so clean and empty she was afraid, as though she was on a glass stage, especially with the cameras installed on the cracked-plaster walls.

"Remember not to look, but there's a camera in here," whispered Alois to Levi.

"Aw now, Smokie. What if I git happy in my pants?" whispered Levi, pinching Alois on the bottom.

Alois swatted his hand away. "We ain't a-gonna end up on some triple X movie."

She couldn't remember the last time she had slept in a bed that was off the floor. Her husband peeled out of his dinner jacket and started to toss it on the floor. She hooked her hand under his arm and pulled him out of the room, down the hall, and into the women's restroom.

"I didn't mean tonight, Smokie. I'm a little tuckered out," said Levi.

Alois closed the door and checked the walls for cameras. None. Several clawfoot tubs lined one wall, and toilets behind wooden stalls lined the other wall. A stack of chamber pots sat on a table near the door.

"Now listen here, Levi. We're supposed ta be all uptown now. Ya can't go an' throw your clothes on the floor anymore," whispered Alois. "Besides, we're being filmed everywhere we go—except to pee."

"There weren't no closet in our room," said Levi.

"That fancy cabinet in our room is what they use for closets here," whispered Alois. She giggled behind her hand. "Oh, Levi! Can you believe how nice our room is?"

"Yeah, yeah," huffed Levi. "Well, I ain't gonna keep bein' nice to that Millie woman if she keeps talking bad about my maw—I mean 'my mum,'" he said, after Alois looked sideways at him.

"Since when have you started telling the truth? You shouldn't've told Millie she was worldly and Hell-bound no matter who said it. We might get sent back to Mississippi and have to live under a bridge at this point."

CHAPTER SIX

Despite the camera in the bedroom, Alois slept better than she had expected on her clean sheets and pillows. And best of all, she didn't have to worry about any critters crawling on her. She was so comfortable, she turned over and wanted to continue in her cloud of comfort, but someone knocked on the door. Before she could step out of bed and get her new robe from the cabinet, the three servants entered the bedroom.

"Millie doesn't tolerate lateness," said Ms. Johns, standing starchy in her uniform.

"Lateness?" asked Alois. She covered herself with her pillow and scooted sideways toward the wardrobe.

"You won't be needing anything from the wardrobe. I know it must seem degrading for a lord and lady, but you and your husband will be wearing *these* from now on," said Mr. Shaw, handing Alois some garments on two wire coat hangers. He exchanged bright-eyed glances with the other servants.

Levi covered himself in the sheet and stood beside his wife to inspect their new clothes. One hanger supported a woman's pale-gray cotton dress and white apron and a matching white bonnet, which matched Ms. John's uniform. On the other hanger was a brown tweed vest, trousers, and a tweed cap, as well as a white cotton shirt and simple tie, which matched Taylan's clothing.

"Oh, what a relief," said Levi, taking his hanger. "We were afraid we'd soil our clothes—um, what with the house being repaired and all."

"Ears," said Alois in her new sophisticated accent, taking her hanger. "Plaster dust is nearly impossible to remove from clothing, I'm afraid." She loved the fancy new clothes Derick bought her but was desperate to feel comfortable again.

Taylan's snigger vanished, and he looked at the older servants as if confused.

"Where might I find Lady Pimbledon this morning? I'm rather eager to speak with her," said Alois. She was determined to get Millie to like her family.

"I'm sure you're unhappy with your rooms and all, but Lady Pimbledon is preoccupied with her morning prayer at the moment," said Ms. Johns. "Now, get dressed and meet us downstairs."

As the servants exited the room, Alois swore she heard one of the servants stifle a snort. Levi and Alois went to the restrooms to change then rejoined in the hall. Levi stretched and did a few squats as if he had finally gotten free of a suit of armor.

"Stop that," whispered Alois, swatting Levi. "We had better wake the children." She turned the glass knob to enter the children's room. It was empty, and the beds had been made as neat as a store-bought birthday present. Alois panted from fear. Her children had never decluttered their mattresses, much less had ever learned to make a bed. Had the pedophile lizard people abducted her children?

"Where's Tara-Belle and Presley? What've they done with our young'uns?"

Alois forgot her accent and that there were cameras in the children's room as well. She felt so inadequate as a parent, and this fancily run mansion made her feel plumb worthless. Was she becoming more and more paranoid? After spending most of her life in a crumbling shack, she was sure she was hallucinating.

"They're probably outside messing around," said Levi, as they rushed down the back stairs while being followed by a camerawoman and lighting crew.

"And here they come crawling out of bed at this hour—shameful," said Mr. Shaw, standing against the wall beside the other two servants and Alois's children, who were dressed in mini uniforms just like Alois and her husband—just like the servants.

Ms. Johns shoved a mop into Alois's hand. Taylan handed Levi a pair of hedge trimmers.

"Look, Alois. They got us gifts," said Levi, frowning at the trimmers.

"Oh dear. I'm frightfully embarrassed to say we didn't get you anything," said Alois.

"You'll return those tools to us at the end of each day," said Ms. Johns, with her chin jutted. "Look, Mr. and Mrs.

Gurney, I'm sure your family is used to having a staff doing everything for you. But Lady Pimbledon doesn't trust any old workers to repair this estate."

"She has a fear of being robbed by the working class," whispered Mr. Shaw. "A woman of her standing can't be too careful these days."

"That's, uh, right. And Lady Pimbledon is a real traditionalist when it comes to uniforms," said Taylan.

"Excuse us for a moment," said Levi. Putting his hand behind his wife's back, he guided her behind the staircase. Alois was sure she heard another snicker from the servants and not a squeaky wooden step.

"You were right, Alois. Derick and Suki—they done gone and tricked us," whispered Levi. "They are making us servants."

"Oh now, Levi," said Alois behind her cupped hand. "This is going to be our house soon. Maybe they expect us to help restore it, ya know. We can't refuse—not with the whole world watching. Maybe this is how these reality shows work—ya know, like a contest or game show.

"Or maybe all these here cameras are to keep us from escaping," said Levi.

"Okay, let's just calm down. If it gets to be too much, I'll talk to Derick or Suki as soon as I can and see what's going on here," said Alois.

"Lots of work to be done," said Taylan, rounding the corner with the crew, startling Alois. "Best get going." The young gardener ordered Levi and Presley to follow him out the back door of the manor house.

"You and Tara-Belle come with me," Ms. Johns said to Alois, walking them to the sprawling kitchen where pots and pans hung everywhere. Tara-Belle ran around the kitchen, asking what everything was.

"Mummy, Mummy, are these greens?" She pointed to a bunch of peppers and onions on a tray.

"Greens? Are you sure you don't mean vegetables?" asked Ms. Johns, with a pinched face. "Anyway, you both will mop the rooms on the first two floors, and I'll mop the top two floors. You will toss your bucket water out the back door and refill it here in this sink."

"How many rooms are there in this house?" asked Alois.

"Therapon Hall has over one hundred and thirty rooms," replied Ms. Johns. She lingered behind a cabinet for a few seconds, then placed a bottle of floor cleaner on the big table in the middle of the kitchen. She grabbed a bucket of water and headed up the back steps.

Alois carried her bucket to the library, where she and her daughter gazed around at the high shelves all around the room and smaller shelves near the center. All leather-bound books with embossed and gold-lettered spines and not a paperback in sight.

"Can I have a book, Mummy?" asked Tara-Belle.

"Maybe later," said Alois, pushing her mop over the beautiful wooden floor near a library table. "I've been meaning to ask. Did you and Presley clean your own room?"

"Ears. Ms. Johns showed us how," said Tara-Belle,

pulling the bucket closer to Alois as she began mopping near curved stairs. Then Tara started playing with the bottle of soap.

"What's happening to the floor?" gasped Alois. She looked at the head of her mop and then in the bucket; it was as red as the floor where she had just mopped. "It's turning to blood! I knew it. This is the devil's house!"

"I don't think so, Mummy," said Tara-Belle, while the cameraman zoomed in on the red stains.

"What do you mean? Can't you see the blood? They probably sacrifice children in this room." Alois dropped her mop handle.

Tara-Belle pulled a bottle out of her apron pocket and showed her mother. Alois snatched it out of her hand. "Oh, Tara-Belle, did you put red ink in the bottle of soap?"

"No, Mummy. I saw Ms. Johnses put it in the bottle, and then I tooked it."

Alois examined the bottle of soap. Sure enough, it was as red as blood, and a thin stream of red dribbled down the side of the bottle.

"You took it? You mean she put ink in the soap. But why?"

"I dunno." Tara-Belle shrugged.

"You empty the bucket. We have to do something, or Millie is going to kill us." Alois ran back to the kitchen and opened the cabinet, flinging cleaning products everywhere, until she found a bottle of rubbing alcohol. She flung open another closet and grabbed a handful of dishrags before running back to the library. She blotted as much of the ink and water up with the rags as she could, and then she poured the alcohol on the wet stains. After two repeats of this process, the floor had returned to its beautiful golden-brown colors, but Alois was dripping in sweat. When she and Tara-Belle had finished the bottom floor, Alois caught Mr. Shaw peeking into the room while holding a dust cloth.

"Mr. Shaw," yelled Alois, before lowering her voice as she had been taught.

"Good heavens, what? Did something happen? Are you having trouble?"

"No," Alois lied. "I was—well, I was wondering if you knew of any way I could get Lady Pimbledon to warm up to me. I don't think she is too fond of us."

Mr. Shaw's eyes kept darting at the floors throughout the mansion. "You might try asking her about her late husband. She loves to talk about him and how he died."

"I don't ever see her. Can you tell her I would like to speak to her?"

"I'll try," he said. "Now, if you'll excuse me, I have to check on the delivery schedule."

"Certainly. Thanks. Pip-pip," said Alois, lifting her mop before the butler walked toward the kitchen.

The grandfather clock in the study struck five that afternoon. Alois and Tara-Belle finally finished mopping the second floor without anyone asking them to stop for lunch. She wasn't even sure if the Gurneys would be having dinner with Millie each night, as they had when they arrived at the estate. Tara-Belle was whining at this point, popping bubbles in the dirty mop water with her toes.

Alois grabbed the mop and bucket, and they returned to the kitchen to find the three servants had finished their dinner and were putting their plates into the sink.

"Finished finally, are we?" asked Ms. Johns, sucking food from her teeth. The smell of roast beef and fresh bread made Alois's stomach churn from hunger.

"Ms. Johns, may I ask why you poured red ink into our bottle of floor cleaner?" asked Alois, trying to keep calm, as the spotlights around her caused her to sweat worse.

"I'm afraid I have no idea of what you are talking about, Mrs. Gurney." Ms. Johns pushed her glasses back up her snarling nose when Levi and Presley came staggering into the kitchen, covered in mud. "Why would I put ink in the soap?"

"You must have. Tara-Belle saw you do it," said Alois, while Levi and Presley froze at the edge of the kitchen.

Ms. Johns jerked away from the rubbish bin. "Mrs. Gurney, I am Lady Pimbledon's longest surviving maid. I assure you I have no intentions of violating her trust by ruining her floors with . . . ink." Her voice softened, and she offered a slight smile. "Perhaps that girl of yours did it. You know how children are."

Shaking, Alois didn't want to show her emotions in front of her family. She needed some confirmation that she wasn't losing her mind—that she remembered things the way they had happened. "Mr. Shaw," said Alois, rushing up to him and easing her hand on his black jacket. "Were you able to speak with Lady Pimbledon?"

"I did, Mrs. Gurney." Mr. Shaw smiled and gave a slight bow. "She doesn't feel up to talking, I'm afraid. Perhaps some other day." He wiped his mouth with his napkin and placed his dessert plate in the sink. Alois and her family watched longingly as the metal lid closed over the roast, and Taylan put it in the icebox.

"Now, out, all of you!" said Ms. Johns, shooing everyone out of the kitchen. She grabbed a turkey breast out of the icebox and unwrapped the plastic around it. "I need to prepare Lady Pimbledon's dinner. She requested penguin."

Alois stopped cold in the doorway with her husband. "And I suppose you're going to claim you are serving us penguin meat tonight. I clearly saw the wrapper labeled 'turkey,'" said Alois, glad to catch the maid in an obvious lie.

"Lady Pimbledon has not included you or your family as diner guests tonight," said Ms. Johns with a smug grin. "She will be dining as she always does, just her, her husband, and her poodle."

"I thought her husband was dead," said Levi.

"He is," said Taylan, cutting his eyes at the other two servants.

Ms. Johns nodded at the butler, and he popped a cooking pan over the camera mounted high on the wall. She shoved her hands on her hips and strutted up to Alois. "Look, Gurney family, you all had better learn this and learn it fast," Ms. Johns said in a lower voice. "Lady Pimbledon always gets her way, even if it's not possible or legal. You use whatever means you have to keep her happy, even if it means dyeing a chicken pink and soaking it in fish broth to make it taste like a bloody flamingo. Do we have an understanding?"

"I see," said Alois in disbelief at how spoiled Millie was and at the way her family was being treated.

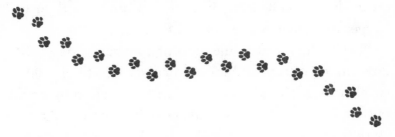

After the fourth week had passed, Alois was outside the manor house, raking grass and leaves from the gravel drive while Levi scrubbed mildew stains off the marble statues in the formal gardens. For many nights, Alois and her family had gathered in her bedroom to watch The Benefactrix. Alois and Levi couldn't believe how the show's producers were pitting everyone in the manor house against one another. Alois hardly recognized herself or her family on television with their new looks and accents. In fact, she wouldn't be able to stand the new Gurneys if she had met them six weeks earlier. Worst of all, gossip and speculations about her family were now roaring like fire through the estate and across the country. And if that weren't enough, Derick and Suki had returned to the United States to work on promotions for the reality show there, or so they claimed.

Alois gritted her teeth, worrying about everything. She felt a sharp pain in her jaw on the bottom right side. A couple of her teeth had broken in half. When the cameras had panned away, she spat out her rotted teeth along with a handful of blood. She had never been able to afford dental visits and certainly couldn't now. She dropped her rake and broken teeth when Levi fell headfirst into the statue before collapsing into the primrose and formal hedges that encircled the yellow flowers.

"Levi!" she yelled, while running toward the statue. She dove on top of Levi and rolled him over. His forehead had swollen an inch, and there was a small cut bleeding on the puffy mound that had formed above his left eye. "Are you all right, dear?"

"I'm fine," groaned Levi. He reached to cup his hand over the cut, and his whole arm shook. The camera crew surrounded the scene, filming every second of it. Alois couldn't hold back. There was nowhere for them to hide—to discuss their plans privately or do anything for that matter.

Alois cupped her hand behind his head. "That's it! You are going to have to stop, Levi. We didn't come here to be Millie's servants. She is working you like a dog. Your condition is getting worse."

"There's nothing wrong with me—nothing a'tall." Levi's face screwed up, an expression Alois took as a warning not to continue discussing the matter. But how much longer could her husband hold out before his ALS symptoms became impossible to hide?

"We should get you to a doctor at least. You might need stitches," said Alois, while her son Presley stumbled to the scene covered in so many vines, he looked like a walking bush. Tara-Belle and her dog were helping pick up sticks and moving them to a pile to be burned.

"I ain't gonna go to no doctor," whispered Levi. "They might trace my medical records and know about my condition. Millie might know where we're from."

"Is Mr. Gurney hurt? Is he going to be leaving Therapon Hall?" panted Taylan Chowdhury, the young gardener, running up to Levi with his shovel. His dark eyes enlarged, and bushy eyebrows disappeared behind his black bangs.

"Don't be daft, young man," said Alois in her most posh drawl. "Lord Gurney is going to apologize to the statue for hurting its feelings, and then tomorrow, he is going to continue restoring this awfully neglected house."

Later that night, Alois's mouth throbbed from teeth pain, and Levi still had a headache from the fall, so she wrapped herself in her sleeping robe and eased out of her bedroom. She made her way to the kitchen, where she was luckily alone. In the cabinet next to the sink, Alois found the pot of gold at the end of the rainbow—a whole bottle of over-the-counter pain pills. She filled a glass with water and swallowed a handful of the medicine before placing a few gold nuggets for Levi in her robe pocket.

Tiptoeing back into the great hall, Alois dodged behind the edge of the servants' staircase. A woman in a blue hooded robe was standing in the middle of the hall, lifting a lit candle over her head as though she were looking for a bat flying near the ceiling.

"Wilfred? Wilfred, if you're there, I know you loved that baby girl, but we were hungry. We had to obey the ruling class," sobbed Millie. "Don't hate me, not now. We both did what he had to do to survive—to preserve our heritage, our estate."

Alois's blood heated. Had she taken too many pain pills?

"Oh, sweet baby Jaysus! Millie and her dead husband are rotten' stinkin' baby eaters! They're lizard shapeshifters," Alois whispered under her panicking breath.

Millie wasn't looking for no bat. Alois realized she was looking for a lizard or praying to Satan. Alois should've known Millie was a part of the Illuminati, the ruling class who were taking over the world until people like Alois and other red-blooded patriots destroyed them in The Storm. To her, the signal from "Q" and the president to begin the day of judgment couldn't come fast enough now—unless Alois took matters into her own hands before then.

CHAPTER SEVEN

Alois and Levi awoke and found a newspaper on the floor outside their door. Their eyes settled on the photograph of the Gurney family, which took up most of the page under the headline: SOMETHING'S DISTURBING ABOUT THE GURNEYS. Alois's heart beat erratically as she sat on the edge of her freshly made bed and read the article.

"Well, are you reading it or not? What does the blasted paper say?" asked Levi, pacing the floor with a dark bruise on his forehead.

Alois crumpled the newspaper in her hands. "Nothing of grave importance. A bunch of ridiculous gossip, really." She lifted her face to the cameras and faked a calm smile. She couldn't let the whole world see her upset and know they were getting to her. And most of all, she didn't want to upset Levi in his condition. Most of the article focused on Levi and how his speech and behavior were suspiciously common to be a true lord. Reporters also had been digging for information about the Gurneys and claimed none of the aristocracies in Wadebridge, England, had ever heard of Levi or Alois. And the reporters claimed the producers of The Benefactrix were blocking their news teams from getting more information on the Gurneys, especially the exact location of their alleged estate in southern England. "Lord and Lady of the Rings," the article declared, suggesting that perhaps the Gurneys had been living as halflings underground all these years.

"Well, who left that rubbish outside our door?" snorted Levi. "It had to be one of the servants."

"Pay it no thought, Levi dear. We have to get to work now." Alois took her uniform and headed to the women's restroom to change. When her husband passed by the restroom door, Alois snatched him inside.

"I've been thinking," said Alois. "What if this reality show is all a test. I mean, it's been a month, and we haven't even seen Millie. If we pissed her off that bad, ya'd think she would've sent us packing." She had made up her mind not to tell her husband about Millie being with the Illuminati. He hated when she discovered a new truth or clue, which he called one of her conspiracy theories.

Levi pressed his back against the door to keep anyone from entering. "*Ermph*, she's pissed a'ight. She even told the servants to stop calling us by our fancy titles. I know you women want your fairy-tale castle and all, but she's using us for free labor, then she's gonna kick us out. Old Millie's even got me fishin' her turds out of her toilet and putting them in the dirt around her heirloom roses."

"You gotta be pulling my leg, Levi! What the hell for?"

"Fertilizer, I reckon."

"Well, I never," Alois shook her head. "She must think

she shits gold bricks or something."

Levi stumbled forward with a loud thud. In the doorway stood Ms. Johns with two burly film assistants who stood in the opening with folded arms and frowns.

"Just as I told you," Ms. Johns said to the men. She stood behind them with her arms folded and a smug grin while more film crew squeezed in with cameras and lighting.

"Mr. Gurney, need we inform you that men are not allowed in the women's lavatory?" said the beefiest of the two men. "You and Alois have violated your contract: the stars of The Benefactrix are not allowed to communicate in private. If it happens again, we will have to report you to production."

"Oh, don't be absurd," said Alois. "My husband and I can't have a moment to discuss a private matter? What do you imagine we're doing—plotting to escape this dungeon of misery?"

"Lady Pimbledon will be most displeased. She may have to move you to the virgins' wing, Mrs. Gurney," said Ms. Johns.

"Why, I wouldn't dream of intruding on your territory, Ms. Johns," said Alois, plowing through the barricade of people with Levi behind her. She could still sense the psychotic twitch of the maid's right eye on her.

After a quiet breakfast of toast and tea, the Gurneys began their daily work assignments. Tara-Belle kept running in and out of the sitting room and hiding behind the antique furniture. Alois tried to ignore her while she continued brushing the Persian rugs as she had been instructed. She had been on all fours for so long she felt like a cow in a pasture. A shadow coming from the hall startled her. It was Mr. Shaw.

"Mrs. Gurney, when you are finished here, the silver needs cleaning. Oh, and do be careful; Lady Pimbledon is quite fond of her collection. It originally belonged to the family of Queen Victoria."

"What do I clean it with?" asked Alois.

"The cleaning kit is in the utility room closet by the back stairs. Make sure you get the kit on the right, next to the dustpan."

"Oh, before you leave," said Alois. "I was wondering if you might know whether Lady Pimbledon ever had children?"

"Not that I am aware," said Mr. Shaw, inspecting the rug.

"Might I ask you a question, Mrs. Gurney?"

"Certainly," said Alois.

"I suppose it's no secret that Lady Pimbledon found Levi's mother to be unappreciative for helping her. We servants often feel the same. I was just wondering if Levi's mother was truly happy with her decision to turn her back on her mother and Lady Pimbledon."

Alois tried to remember any discussions of Levi's parents.

"I can't say for certain," she said. "But from everything I remembered about the Mary Gurney, she was never happy about much of anything."

"Hmm," Mr. Shaw mumbled before leaving the sitting room. Alois headed toward the back stairs with a forward tilt in her posture now.

"I guess he meant the laundry room," Alois said to Tara-Belle. This room had an old sink with ceramic jugs and wicker baskets on the shelves above it, a row of washers and dryers to her right, and ironing boards near the linen closet. She opened the closet near an old washtub and on the floor was a wooden box with a handle on the top. "This must be the kit; it's the only one by the dustpan, but I don't see the other kit he mentioned." She opened the box and saw a bottle marked nitric acid, a scrub brush, and thick rubber gloves. "This doesn't seem right. Of course, I've never polished silver before."

"Mr. Shaw hadded a box like that one," said Tara-Belle. "He putted it under the chair in the hall."

"Why would Mr. Shaw put the other kit under a chair? Show me which one," said Alois, taking her daughter's hand and returning to the great hall. Tara-Belle stopped walking and pointed to a heavily upholstered chair, where the fabric overlapped its four legs. She lifted a flap, and sure enough, there was a near-exact box to the one in her left hand. She opened the box and felt as though she had been hit in the stomach. Inside was a clearly marked bottle of silver polish, cloth gloves, and a polishing cloth. She looked again at the bottle of nitric acid in her box. "Warning! Highly corrosive. Causes severe burns."

"Oh my God!" Alois gasped. "The servants really are trying to get us in trouble—trying to turn Millie against us. I'm going to switch the boxes. Won't they all be stunned when they see the silver isn't ruined?"

Alois remained in the dining hall until she had polished all the silver in the china cabinet, on the dining table, and on the sideboard. Her arms were about to fall off, but the silver looked like it was made of mirrors now. She could see the entire room reflected on the tea pitcher. It was quite hypnotic. She jumped when she heard crying in the hall; it was her son, Presley. He was flinging his arms wildly while Levi chased after him.

"What happened?" asked Alois, tearing into the hall.

"Presley got stung by a slew of hornets," said Levi, trying to get Presley to be still.

"Argh! It's Taylan's fault," sobbed Presley. "He told me to—to climb that tree and cut the limbs."

"I didn't know the tree had a hornets' nest. I can't help it if he's too stupid to see where he's climbing," sneered Taylan, the gardener.

"Take him to the kitchen and put some ice on the stings," said Alois, when Mr. Shaw came down the grand stairs.

"I heard someone crying. The ointment for burns is in the kitchen drawer," said Mr. Shaw, looking at Alois's hands, and then he stuck his head in the dining room, and Alois knew he was checking to see how terribly she had damaged the silver service.

"Mr. Shaw, what made you think I got burned? The crying you heard was my son—he got a bunch of hornet stings."

The butler turned a sicker shade of pasty, and his neck reddened. "Well, I just assumed. I, uh—"

"You assumed that nitric acid you wanted me to polish the silver with had burned me—that's why you hid the real polishing kit under that chair over there." Alois pointed across the great hall.

Mr. Shaw cleared his throat and glared over his bulbous nose at her. "Mrs. Gurney, these unfounded accusations need to stop. We do not need the police showing up here and upsetting Lady Pimbledon. In her condition, it would be the end of her."

Alois saw the cameras mounted on the wall near the crown molding and decided to take a gamble. "Unfounded? Is that so? Well, the production staff caught it on camera. They told me themselves."

The butler gnawed on his clenched lips and finally exhaled through flaring nostrils.

"Oh, that," he said with a cracking voice. "You mean I put the wrong kit under the chair?" Mr. Shaw reached under the chair and removed the box.

"Yes, you did," said Alois. "Luckily, I found it before ruining Lady Pimbledon's silver."

"It was a mistake, of course. I . . . I didn't want to risk any accidents," continued the butler. "During my twenty years of service here, I have seen my share of mishaps. One can't be too careful, I'm afraid."

"Maybe the staff should ease up with all their carefulness," said Alois, before Mr. Shaw took both kits back to the utility room.

The front doors to the estate opened, and Millie came strutting into the hall in her Sunday hat, gloves, and swanky dress. She had something close to a smile on her face for the first time.

"Lady Pimbledon, I need to have a word with you," said Alois. She tried to look beneath the woman's makeup to see if her skin was green or scaly. But she really wanted to reach out and strangle her.

"I suppose," Millie replied. "But do be careful not to spoil my mood. The Holy Spirit is still holding me in its glowing embrace. He-he-he!" she giggled, and her hat wobbled when she lifted her chin and batted her eyelashes at the cameraman.

"It's just—well, I'm concerned about my family's safety," said Alois, lowering her voice. "Your servants keep setting traps for us. I nearly got burned. Of course, Mr. Shaw now claims it was a mistake on his part. And that gardener of yours nearly got my son killed by hornets."

"Don't stress, dear woman. It upsets my digestion," sighed Millie, with her hand over her pearls.

"Oh? I'll bet you need some more baby's blood for that digestion of yours." Alois thought she would pass out. She couldn't believe she had let her anger cause her to say such a thing.

"What?" asked Millie, while a camera lens expanded between them.

"I, uh, mean blood pudding—the kind they, uh, serve babies," said Alois, certain her neck had turned redder.

"Dependable people are so hard to find. At this last

stage in my life, I need people to get along and do their jobs. I'm hopeful that your family will be here until the end. I need to leave all of this to my most loyal after all." Millie's hand fluttered in a quick sweep around her head.

Feeling Millie was finally warming to her, Alois remembered what Mr. Shaw suggested she try in order to befriend her. "I guess I just get a bit emotional when it comes to my family. I'm sure you know what it's like, losing your husband and all. How did he die, may I ask?"

"Wuh! Of all the nerve. How dare you inquire of my husband's death!" Millie turned her head with a snap and headed for the grand staircase, spouting scriptures the entire way: "The tongue is a restless evil, full of deadly poison. . . . If anyone thinks he is religious and does not bridle his tongue, this person's religion is worthless. . . . It's not what enters into the mouth that defiles the man, but what proceeds out of the mouth!"

Alois stood in the great hall in a state of disbelief. Surely, she had ruined any chances the Gurneys had of receiving their inheritance. One thing for certain, Alois would never again trust Mr. Shaw or the other servants— not even to hand her a toothpick.

CHAPTER EIGHT

The next morning, Alois was sure her kneecaps would be permanently smashed before she would finish scrubbing the baseboards in the hall outside Millie's bedroom. She knew Millie was making her chores harder to punish her, but she probably deserved it for asking about how her husband died, and the Gurneys had come too far to quit now. Alois's son, Presley, was on his knees, scrubbing the baseboard closest to the bedroom door. Alois peeked inside the bedroom; Millie had closed the velvet curtains around her canopy bed to shut out the light. No alarm clock in sight.

The film crew recorded Taylan, who guided them through the hall while holding a bouquet of pastel-colored roses he had freshly cut from the gardens.

"I'm the only person Lady Pimbledon trusts to cut her heirloom roses," whispered Taylan, who had worn a nicer vest and shirt than usual and had neatened his hair. "Every week, part of my job is to select the best blooms, and then I am to place them in the Ming dynasty vase on her bedroom pedestal. That way, it's the first thing she sees when she wakes up every morning.

"Like a proper sniff, would you?" Taylan asked the man interviewing him. With a naughty sparkle in his eyes, he held a pink rose to the man's nose, and he took a sniff and then jerked his head back with a pinched face.

"Now, we have to be very quiet because Her Ladyship is still sleeping," continued Taylan. "She's not been at all well since the Gurneys upset her so. No manners at all with that lot."

Cradling the roses in his arms, Taylan kicked Presley's foot out of the doorway before entering Millie's bedroom.

"Don't you ever talk about my family like that," said Presley, climbing to his feet, holding his washcloth. "And don't kick me ever again. My hornet stings are still sore."

"Remember what I told you, Presley. Just ignore him," said Alois. She motioned for him to calm down and get back to work.

"Those aren't hornet stings; they're pimples? Maybe if you bathed more often, you wouldn't look like a pork pie," Taylan said to Presley, while he arranged the flowers in the vase.

"Shut up, or I'm gonna kick your ass!" yelled Presley.

Alois's stomach knotted. Presley had said the word "ass" instead of the British "arse." And worst of all, it sounded much more impolite in his Mississippi accent.

"My what?" laughed Taylan, cleaning up the fallen leaves and rose petals around the vase. "Say, are you a Yank? Where are you people from?"

"I could ask the same about you," hissed Presley.

"What—because of my skin color?" asked Taylan,

shoving him until Presley pushed back, and the two began punching each other with their fists. After receiving a hard smack on the nose, Taylan fell backward onto a mannequin wearing a beautiful white gown, and before she could break up the fight, Alois heard the sound of a long jagged rip. The film crew moved faster and whipped their cameras around, trying to keep up with the boys.

Millie flung open the curtains on her bed. "What is the meaning of this beastly disturbance?" She wrapped a pink robe around herself and squeezed her bare feet into a pair of feathery pink slippers.

Taylan held his shirt cuff over his bleeding nose. "I'm sorry, Your Ladyship. Presley here threw a wobbler when I was arranging your flowers. A right dim git he is."

"He attacked me first," wheezed Presley, while climbing off the mannequin. The dress was now ripped in half down the front, and it crumpled to the floor.

"You have ruined my famous dress!" said Millie. She patted her hair into place as the cameraman focused the huge lens on her. "When I was eighteen, my aunt presented me before Queen Elizabeth II's Court in that white dress and those gloves. I attended the social season—went to more tea parties and balls than I could count. Little did I know that little old me, Millie S. Pimbledon, would be the last debutante ever to be presented in the queen's court." Millie brushed her fingertips across her upper chest. "You see, the other girls were so jealous—made a spectacle of themselves in front of Elizabeth and the media. The queen had to abolish the ceremony because of that. Naturally, I insisted she think nothing of it. Mind you, some of those girls had a debutante ball for two or more seasons. Such poor taste, I say."

"We're so very sorry, Lady Pimbledon. Perhaps— perhaps the dress can be mended," said Alois. She rushed farther into the room and lifted the mannequin back into place. The deeply frayed edges of the delicate white fabric suggested the dress was now doomed for dust rags.

"Mrs. Gurney, make no mistake; this is your fault and, and that boy of yours. You all are like those jealous girls who put an end to the queen's court. I'm afraid your inheritance is not looking too promising."

Over his bloody sleeve, Taylan's eyes settled on Presley and Alois with a sneaky sparkle.

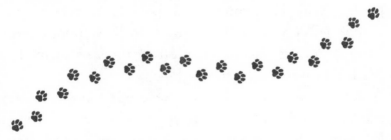

In the greenhouse after lunch, Alois cornered Presley behind a plant with coin-shaped leaves. Workers were on a forklift, installing new glass where the panes had broken.

"Son, why didn't you ignore Taylan?" whispered Alois. She grabbed Presley's shovel before he scooped another heap of dirt from a mound and dumped it in a clay pot.

Presley lowered his head. "Ah, Maw. Taylan's just like the kids from my school back home. I get tired of getting picked at all the time. I thought if I looked like I wasn't poor anymore—if I was in another country—things would change. Aw, Maw, why do I gotta have pimples and be so dumb?"

"You'll grow out of acne, and you aren't dumb, Son," said Alois. "You just need to learn to have pride in yourself and keep working with your tutor. It's not how rich you are or having good skin. It's what's inside that makes you special." She laughed, feeling a bit of pride in Presley. "Besides, you just put a boy at least four years older than you in his place this morning. I'll bet old Taylan won't bother you again."

"Is Millie gonna make us leave?" asked Presley, lifting his head a little.

"That I don't know. I saw her walking outside in her garden. Why don't you go and apologize to her? Ask her if she's got any pictures of herself in that famous dress. Women always like to show off pictures of themselves when they were younger."

Alois would prefer Presley curse out a possible baby eater like Millie instead of apologizing to her. Still, Alois kept reminding herself of the money and property her family stood to inherit. Millie would soon get the ending she deserved.

"*Mumph.* Do I gotta go out there by myself?"

"No, I'll go with you," said Alois. She adjusted Presley's tweed cap and vest, and they walked out of the greenhouse, past the butterfly conservatory, and toward Millie, who was now sitting on a stone bench under a shade tree. Her poodle bounced at Millie's feet and growled whenever the Gurney's hound dog got too close.

"Go ahead. You can do it," said Alois, pushing her son closer to the bench, while she gave the two of them a bit of distance. She struggled not to stare while Presley inched in the shadows of the film crew on his way toward Millie.

"What do you want? Don't you have work to do?" asked Millie.

"I'm s-sorry about your dress, Lady Pimbledon. You could show me a picture of you in it if you want to," stammered Presley, while a crowd of people gathered behind the gates of the property. Many took photos and shouted out the Gurneys' names.

"Your mum put you up to this, did she not?" huffed Millie. She lifted her chin and, with a snort, turned her back to Presley.

"Yes, Lady Pimbledon, but I, I do want to apologize for—"

Millie unfolded her arms and pivoted back around toward the boy. "Now you get out of my sight and get back to—"

Millie froze and looked up with her mouth ajar when a news reporter and the crowd burst through the gate and ran toward her. She fluffed the scarf around her neck and straightened the diamond brooch of her family crest. The radiance that had popped up on her face melted when the crowd swarmed around Alois and Presley instead of her. Millie staggered a bit before turning to face her sprawling estate as though she was just getting some sun and air.

"Hey! Can we have your autograph?" asked a young girl with green hair, handing Presley photos of him. Another girl broke through the crowd, holding a pen and a t-shirt. She spoke in a language Alois couldn't recognize. Neither of the two gals was anything close to what Alois wanted near her son. But after seeing the blush fade from Presley's cheeks and a stunned smile light his face, she wouldn't dare spoil that experience for him, even if the girls were no doubt Godless.

A large woman, wearing a red and blue t-shirt with the cast of The Benefactrix printed across the front and back, pointed her finger at Millie. "Lady Pimbledon, you and your servants had better stop being mean to the Gurneys. They deserve the inheritance. We're watching you. We see everything going on in Therapon Hall!"

The reporter shoved his microphone under Millie's upturned nose. "Lady Pimbledon, is it true that you are, in fact, turning the Gurneys into servants and have no plans on leaving them their promised inheritance?"

"Guards!" Millie shouted, jumping up from the bench and pushing through the fans with her yipping poodle in hand. "Get these horrid people off my property. How dare you? How dare you?" Millie wobbled toward her mansion, muttering loudly: "'Sin is not ended by multiplying words, but the prudent hold their tongues. . . . A gossip betrays a confidence, but a trustworthy person keeps a secret. . . . All my enemies whisper together against me; they imagine the worst for me. . . .'"

That evening, after the Gurney family had finished

their chores and had greeted fans, they took the back servants' staircase to their rooms. In the hall, Mr. Shaw paused with his cleaning cart he had been pushing. A camera operator stood six feet behind him.

"Might I have a word with you all?" he asked.

The Gurneys all paused.

"Lady Pimbledon has been most displeased with your conduct. She insists you refrain from talking with the press or with fans. And beginning first thing tomorrow morning, you will start to work repairing the slate shingles on the roof," said Mr. Shaw.

"What? You can't be serious. I'm terrified of heights. She cannot possibly expect my family to climb up on that-there steep roof. It's too dangerous." Alois's voice rose, and her throat constricted.

"Do pardon me, Mrs. Gurney," said Mr. Shaw. "I must be losing my hearing, but did you just say, 'that-there roof'?"

"It's any wonder my wife can even speak at all—expecting us ta fix Lady Pimbledon's roof," said Levi, moving in front of Alois, who stood behind him shaking.

"I'm merely giving you instructions from Lady Pimbledon," said Mr. Shaw. "Very well, I shall inform her you all will be leaving Therapon Hall tomorrow."

"Yeah, you do that!" said Alois, stomping into her room with Levi and slamming the door.

CHAPTER NINE

In the middle of the night, someone cupped their hand over Alois's mouth, pulled her off the mattress and under the bed. Alois stopped her muffled screams when she realized it was her husband.

"What in the hell are you doing, Levi? You scared me to death," panted Alois, after he removed his hand from her mouth.

"I need ta talk to you away from the cameras," whispered Levi. He reached in his pajama pocket and pulled out a folded letter. "I found this shoved under our door. It's a note from somebody. But I can't tell what it says."

Now that Levi had learned to speak all sophisticated and everything, Alois had forgotten that he still couldn't read worth a damn. She took the letter and quickly scanned the cursive handwriting in blue ink.

"It's a letter from Derick, the producer. He said he convinced Mille that we will not be leaving the show," said Alois.

"Well, he's wrong. I ain't having my wife an' kids climbing no castle roof. I ain't," huffed Levi, bumping his head on the wooden support planks under the bed.

"Derick said he has no control over what Millie chooses to do on her own reality show," whispered Alois. "He's convinced she's inches from being dead, and we'll get our inheritance soon if we don't mess nothing up. If we refuse to do the work, it'll turn Millie permanently against us, and we'll be left with nothing."

"Whaddaya mean 'left with nothing,'?" Levi crawled further under the bed.

"Derick said we signed a binding contract, and we'll be sued by production if we back out of it. And there's something else I didn't want to tell you."

"Don't do this to me, Alois. What is it?" With the moonlight beaming through the window, Alois could see her husband wipe beads of sweat off his wrinkled forehead. His eyes seemed to reflect the soul of a crushed man.

"Derick said the town of Wadebridge, Mississippi, seized our property and bulldozed our house down. We got nowhere to go and not one red cent to pay for nothing, Levi."

With a long sigh, Levi lowered his head on the tops of his hands, which now pressed against the cold floor.

"If something happens to you, I don't know what'll happen to me and the kids, Levi. They might put me in prison here with all these foreigners. And I'll lose custody of the children."

"I guess we're gonna be climbing on the roof tomorrow—that's what we're gonna be doing," grunted

Levi.

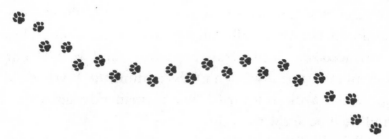

Hardly rested from the previous day's work, Alois and Levi climbed out of bed that morning. With their work uniforms in hand, they headed to the servants' lavatories to shower and dress before breakfast. Even the servants' simple meals were fine dining compared to what the Gurneys could afford back home. And the servants seemed to expect Alois and her family to complain about the meals along with them.

Alois woke her children in their shared bedroom and fished them a fresh uniform each from the wardrobe. Back in the hall, with a camera crew on their heels, Mr. Shaw, Taylan, and Ms. Johns came around the hall corner, snickering and whispering.

"Good morning," said Ms. Johns, jolting into a more professional posture and expression after seeing the Gurney family. "Will you be having a spot of breakfast before you leave. We can help you pack all your things, of course—"

"I can take your uniforms since you won't be needing 'em anymore," said Taylan, with a shifty grin.

Alois jerked her uniform dress out of Taylan's grip. "Who said anything about leaving, silly boy? Indeed. You must be the only Brit incapable of detecting sarcastic humor. But speaking of leaving, are we allowed to leave the estate, you know, to do a little shopping perhaps?"

Ms. Johns eyed the other servants with apprehension. "If there's anything you need, Mrs. Gurney, all you have to do is add it to the list of personal requests by the icebox in the kitchen, and if production approves of it, Mr. Shaw will add it to the inventory."

The sound man behind Ms. Johns dropped his long microphone, and his mouth dropped.

After a breakfast of tea, toast, and black pudding, the Gurneys headed downstairs to begin their work on the roof.

They clung to the hall walls when Millie came toward them, clacking her low heels toward the massive front door. She had on a yellow lace dress and jacket. A veiled yellow hat and matching purse made her resemble a giant canary.

"Move aside," sang Millie. "I have a big offering for the church. The little dears depend on me to keep their doors open." Millie strutted past Alois waving a check in front of the cameras. "We must all be a blessing any way we can."

"I'll pull the car around," said Mr. Shaw.

"Oh, no," said Millie, thrusting out a gloved hand. "I wish to be alone. It'll give me time to make my peace with God. Besides, the exercise will be good for me. I could stand to lose a stone or two before my body lies in state—at Buckingham Palace, I imagine. They can then bury me at St. Paul's, as I have changed my mind about Westminster Abbey. I'll not be buried anywhere close to that Charles Darwin."

"But, Your Ladyship, surely you aren't going to walk all the way," gasped Mr. Shaw.

"Goodness no. Only vulgar pedestrians walk the streets. I'll drive myself. Now clear off."

"As you wish, Your Ladyship," said Mr. Shaw, with a slight bow, before closing the doors behind Millie.

Alois, Levi, Tara-Belle, and Presley peeled themselves from the wall when Taylan Chowdhury motioned for the Gurneys to follow him outside the manor house. They walked past marble statues until they reached a ladder that was as tall as the six floors of the old manor house. Alois stumbled backward while eyeing each rung that seemed to rise into the clouds where the camera drones were hovering like angels. She felt like Jacob in the Bible. But she wasn't sure her family was as special as God's chosen Israelites to be climbing a ladder to Heaven—not when Jesus called Gentiles such as herself "dogs." Alois said a little prayer just in case, while her dog, Sir Eggart Ambrosias Chanticleer, howled at the ladder ominously.

"Are you okay, Mummy?" asked Presley and Tara-Belle, while Levi helped her to her feet.

"Get back." Levi motioned his children away from Alois. "She bumped her head."

"Why all the fuss? I'm all right—simply spiffing really," said Alois, while a camera lens stared down at her unfocused eyes.

"Come on, you bunch of slowcoaches," said Taylan. He took the Gurneys over to the pile of roof slates stacked up beside the ladder. He explained how to look for and remove the deteriorated slates and slide the new ones into place. ". . . And you take your slate hammers and lock it into position with these copper nails and bibs, understand?"

"Yeah, I g-got it, but Tara-Belle is not c-climbing . . . on the roof now. She's too young," Levi stammered, pointing his finger threateningly at Taylan, while a bit of drool trickled from his mouth.

Alois stiffened after seeing her husband's symptoms worsening. This was not comforting her one flea-bottom bit, not when they were about to climb atop the manor house.

Taylan handed Levi a bucket with a long rope tied to the handle. "That's a load of rubbish, it is. That girl of yours is full of beans; she could climb this old ladder easy-peasy!" Taylan's neck bent back when Levi snatched him by his shirt collar, and he dropped the handsaw he had been carrying.

"I'm joking, you twit," wheezed the gardener, before Levi released him. "Tara-Belle can stay right here and fill your bucket with nails and bibs when you run out. Just lower the rope down to her." He thrust the bucket against Levi's stomach, and he took it with trembling hands.

"You look ill. Are you sure you're up to this?" Alois whispered in Levi's ear while the camera crew filmed Presley putting on a tool belt and Tara-Belle playing with the box of nails. Their dog continued to howl.

"I'm fit as a fiddle," whispered Levi, before climbing up the ladder, followed by Presley. Alois took several deep breaths and began her ascent up the ladder. Several windows up, she nearly lost her footing when her uniform apron snagged a protruding nail in the wooden ladder. She gripped the rung above her head and made sure her shoes were positioned squarely on the rung at her feet.

"You can do it, Mummy," Presley called down to Alois, who had no idea how much farther she had to climb; she was too dizzy to look up.

"Presley, how many more steps do I have?" she cried out.

"I can't tell—forty, I guess," yelled Presley, while Tara-Belle's squeals and giggles faded on the ground below them, and the whistle of the wind grew louder.

"Oh, sweet baby Jaysus, catch us—catch us if we fall," Alois muttered and panted as she continued her climb. A drone buzzed by her head, and she nearly screamed when a hand clamped down on her arm.

"You did it, Mummy! Just a little bit more," cheered Presley.

As soon as Alois reached the top, Levi hooked a grass rope around her waist, and the other end looped around one of the dozens of brick chimneys that shot up through the steep roof, which had so many angles, it resembled a dumping ground of discarded pyramids. Presley lay on his stomach at the roof's edge and hoisted up a basket of replacement slates. He had been working so hard, he had lost the extra flab he always carried, and his acne was beginning to clear up. Alois could only guess that it was because they hadn't had any fried food since they left Mississippi.

"How do we know which slates need replacing?" asked Alois, clinging, on her backside, to the steep roof, unlike her two brave men who walked up and down the maze of inclines, inspecting the gray stone shingles.

"If they're cracked or loose, I reckon," said Levi, tapping his knuckles on slates here and there. He carried the basket of slates over to Alois and dropped them behind the chimney where she clung. "You just stay where you are, and don't let this basket slide off the roof."

Alois gladly agreed as her men grabbed a few slates and disappeared over several peaks. Only the occasional hammering assured her they were still alive as she tried to relax and admire the distant English landscape. She hated to admit it, but even the flat fields here were prettier than anywhere she had traveled in the United States. Behind the gates in the distance, she could see the usual crowd of fans gathering and trying to get their attention, which always sent Sir Eggart Ambrosias Chanticleer into a barking frenzy. The dog would shake off his bowtie, hat, and vest the show producers would dress Eggart in for the filming.

For the first time in her life, Alois imagined she was having a taste of what it must feel like to be a movie star. Of course, her lowly upbringing had steered her away from any trappings from that wild lifestyle; those overpaid show people would corrupt a Billy goat as far as Alois was concerned. Still, she couldn't help but wonder if her nosy neighbors back home were watching her on television and that socialist media she's always hearing about. Hell, sure they were. And they were all seething with jealousy over her success—that's why they had bulldozed her house down—those high and might busybodies—why, they wouldn't be anything to look at if they set one foot out of Wadebridge, Mississippi. It had to work; the Gurney family had to receive their inheritance from Millie—that would show her neighbors.

Alois thought she was hallucinating when her eyes settled on the ladder leaning against the edge of the roof. A familiar face was peeping over the top—a tiny face that shouldn't be there.

"TARA-BELLE! What are you doing up here? LEVI—PRESLEY, HELP. Tara-Belle has climbed the ladder!"

Realizing her husband and son couldn't hear her with all the hammering they were doing, Alois released the chimney she had been holding for dear life, and she scooted toward her daughter.

"Tara-Belle, now don't move; stay where you are, and Mummy will come and help you."

"Mummy, look—a hell-copper!" squealed Tara-Belle, pointing, while a drone hovered behind her head, and the crowds down on the ground began to gasp and scream.

"No, baby. That's not a helicopter. Now, don't look at it—you just look at me, okay?"

"'K, Mummy."

Panting heavily, Alois inched closer to her daughter until she was two feet from the roof's edge. She stretched one arm down toward Tara-Belle and heard a scraping and rattling noise. For a second, Alois thought the roof slates had come loose and were somehow causing an avalanche. She looked over her shoulder, and the basket of stone slates had gotten caught in Alois's body rope and had tipped over from behind the chimney and were headed straight toward the top of the ladder—straight at Tara-Belle's head.

"LEVI!" Alois screamed. She flung her legs around, trying to divert the path of the sliding slates. After the third kick of her legs, she toppled backward over the edge of the roof.

After what felt like a half-hour, with her life flashing before her eyes, a gut-crushing squeeze jarred Alois around the waist. Sweet baby Jaysus sure had a painful grip, Alois imagined before she realized the rope had saved her—the rope Levi had hooked around her stomach. High above her head, she could still see slates flying over the edge of the roof, like diving birds, and little Tara-Belle clinging to the ladder for her life. At least her daughter was still hanging on, Alois hoped in agony, seeing double as she swung from the rope upside down, showing the world her new silky drawers, while the bottom of her uniform dress was now tickling her chin.

When her swinging had stilled, she was dangling in front of a window—the window of her and Levi's bedroom. There was no mistaking it was her room because there, on the bed where she had not left her suitcase, was Ms. Johns pilfering through their belongings. And with reddened cheeks, the maid slammed the suitcase shut when she saw Alois hanging outside the window. Their eyes locked.

"Ms. Johns, help me!" Alois cried and waved her arms.

The maid turned toward the door to leave but paused when she spotted, in the wall mirror, the reflection of a drone hovering beside Alois, filming everything. The noise from the crowds behind the fence grew louder. Alois had never felt so helpless in her life. Even if her husband did find her, he would never be able to lift her back up to the roof, not with his muscles deteriorating by the day from his deadly disease. Levi tried to hide the fact that he was having trouble swallowing solid foods by pretending he was only thirsty, and one night he couldn't even swallow a pain pill.

The window opened, and Ms. Johns thrust a broom at her. Good heavens, Alois panicked. Was she trying to swat her out of the air—finish her off?

"I can't reach you. Grab the broom!" yelled Ms. Johns.

Alois grabbed the bristles of the broom, and with a lot of grunting, the maid pulled her close enough to the window that her free hand could grab one of Alois's bare legs and pull her onto the window ledge. She helped free Alois from the rope around her waist and pulled her the rest of the way into the bedroom.

"She's all right. I saved her," Ms. Johns yelled at the drone before closing the window. "You were arse over elbow out there. What happened?"

"Never you mind that. My little girl is up on the ladder. Somebody needs ta help git 'er down," cried Alois, certain the rope and fall had broken her back.

Ms. Johns tapped the side of her cheek with smirking lips. "Hmm, something is rather dodgy about your accent—not getting Southwest England at all. Where have I heard enunciation like that? Yes-yes, I remember—in some Bette Davis movie where they were going to seize her plantation to build a bridge, and she threatened to spit in their eyes."

Alois tried to stand up, but it felt like a knife had stabbed through her spine to her ribs, and she tumbled back on the floor. Did Ms. Johns know about the Gurney's home being bulldozed? "Damn you! Are you deaf? My daughter is in danger."

"Hush, hush, Mrs. Gurney. Clam down. I'll go send someone to help her."

After the maid left the room, Alois managed to get to her feet and hobble over to her suitcase, which still rested on the edge of the bed. She was desperate to see if Ms. Johns had taken anything. God, yes! Her purse had been opened, and all her stuff had been scattered among her personal grooming products.

The bedroom door swung open.

Ms. Johns froze with a guilty expression that Alois could have peeled off the woman's face.

"Mr. Shaw said they've already gotten Tara-Belle down from the ladder safely. Your daughter is simply fine."

Alois placed her hand over her aching heart and steadied her breathing. "Ms. Johns, what were you doing, snooping through my things?" she asked.

The maid gripped her stomach. "Oh, that?" she whispered, cutting her eyes toward the camera mounted on the wall. "I've been a bit nauseous—been running to the loo every ten minutes. I was hoping, woman to woman, that you had some diarrhea medicine. I didn't want anyone to know—it being embarrassing and all." She reached into her apron pocket and removed a key on a ring. "I will be forever in your debt if you would take my car to the nearest chemist and get me some medicine."

Alois couldn't believe Ms. Johns was trusting her to drive her car. The mean old maid must not be as bad as Alois had thought. She did save her from falling—finally.

"I'm not sure I'm in any condition—"

"Nonsense. You owe it to me after saving you," said Ms. Johns.

"How will I know who's a chemist around here and who isn't?" asked Alois, taking the key.

Ms. Johns wrinkled her forehead with suspicion.

"Don't you know what a chemist is, Mrs. Gurney? I do apologize, a lady of your standing—well, of course, you have your staff bring you your medicine. Our nearest chemist is two miles north of here. You can't miss it—across from the old gothic church."

Alois finally realized she was talking about a drugstore, a local title Suki never got around to teaching Alois. But she had no idea England had churches for the strange kids who called themselves goths. She could just picture this demon church now, all black with red stained-glass windows and a pentagram on the roof.

"I'm afraid I don't have any money on me?" said Alois.

"What? A lady of your standing must be dripping in wealth," said Ms. Johns.

"All in the bank," Alois lied. "I just forgot to withdraw a few bits and bobs, you know, for emergencies."

"Just tell them to charge it to Lady Pimbledon. Her staff does all the time," groaned Ms. Johns. "Oops, the rumblies have hit me again. Please hurry with my medicine."

While the maid ran to the lavatory, Alois held the key, steadied her aching back, and headed to the parking garage. Along the way, she checked to see if Tara-Belle was feeling all right.

"We have everything under control, Mrs. Gurney," said Taylan, resting a shovel over his shoulder. "Tara-Belle is over there, playing with that barmy mutt of yours." He aimed the shovel toward the maze of hedges where Tara-Belle was running through the winding paths, giggling and chasing Sir Eggart, who dug a hole under the hedge wall to get to her faster.

Alois exhaled a load of worry. She could see her son and husband, two specks high up on a dormer roof, and she decided to leave for the chemist before she had another panic attack. Perhaps she could charge some pain and nerve pills to Lady Pimbledon as well. She needed it desperately.

When she reached the enormous garage, there were a dozen small cars parked side-by-side. An owl on an overhead rafter turned its head toward her. Alois examined the bird for a minute and concluded that it wasn't a real owl but a camera watching her with big glowing eyes. She laughed quietly: The camera wasn't to keep her or the servants from escaping—surely. Stiff old Mr. Owl up there was to keep people from stealing the cars. Feeling like a burglar herself, Alois waved all nice and friendly at the owl and tried the key on several cars before she finally unlocked a door.

Alois climbed inside before realizing the steering wheels were all on the right side in England. She crawled on hands and knees to the driver's seat and in the car mirror, saw that the owl had turned its head, getting an eyeful of her rear end sticking up. Thankfully, she knew how to use a stick shift, and soon she was on the road, headed north.

She was positive the car trailing behind her with its engine roaring had pulled out of the gates of Therapon Hall seconds after she had. Alois looked in the rearview mirror. Whoever this speed demon was, they were clearly trying to scare her at best. Alois floored the gas pedal and at once was thrust forward a couple of feet after the black car knocked into her pumper. Good thing she had sped up, or her car would have been totaled. She pressed on the horn when a second car was heading straight toward her. She jerked the car into the left lane, narrowly avoiding a head-on collision. Thanks to the oncoming car, the speed demon behind her had to veer off the road, and it smashed into a brick fence instead of finishing her off.

"Argh! Thank goodness I forgot," panted Alois. "These cotton-pickin' nuts drive on the wrong side of the road here." Trembling, she realized pickup trucks were more her speed, but she hadn't seen one since arriving in England.

A mile and a half later, Alois spotted the drugstore across from a dark stone church which was not exactly as she had pictured it but was probably demonic anyway. She carefully pulled into the parking lot. Afraid she might park too close to the other vehicles and get a scratch on the maid's car, Alois parked to the far right of the lot, in front of a narrow lane leading to the garbage dumpster—a beat-up box of metal covered in unreadable words and spray-painted pictures.

It was probably coded messages from the blood-drinking lizard people, Alois imagined.

But something clinging to the dumpster was very out of place—something bright yellow—the ample-sized rear end of a woman in a lace dress. The woman's hatted head popped out of the dumpster, holding what looked like a half-eaten hamburger in a foil wrapper. A brown banana peel hung from the edge of her yellow hat.

"Millie!" gasped Alois, leaning closer to the steering wheel. "What the hell are you doing?"

Alois watched in disbelief as Millie shoved the discarded hamburger in her mouth and crammed what looked like discarded candy bars and other garbage in her yellow purse. Then, after a big swig from a gin bottle,

Millie staggered to her car—another low-sitting car like the one Alois climbed out of, feeling like she had been lying on the ground. In Mississippi, they drove tanks you had to climb inside; it made them feel closer to God, plus it helped them get home faster during rush hour.

She stretched her aching back and looked over at Millie, who was now sitting in front of the steering wheel. Her brassy hair pressed against the driver's window and in her lap was the bottle of gin about to spill on her dress. Alois turned to sneak the long way around her car to reach the drug store entrance but thought of a plan to get in Millie's good graces instead. She opened the front passenger's door.

Millie jumped, nearly spilling gin on herself.

"Lady Pimbledon, you poor dear. Are you okay?"

"Who let you—how did you get here? And how d-dare you break into my car!" sputtered Millie.

Alois patted her on the shoulder. "Look, Lady Pimbledon, your secret is safe with me. I understand. It must be devastating to lose a husband. I'm afraid we'll soon have more in common than you know. But you shouldn't be drinking—not with advanced liver disease."

"I spent a whole month taking my husband's temperature. *Hic.* I spoon-fed that man, and he up and died on me. It was awfully selfish of him—*hic*—awfully."

"Is that what happened to your baby girl?" asked Alois.

"What are you talking about? Wilfred and I were—*hic*—unable to have children."

"I overheard you in the great hall one night; you were

holding a candle and talking to your husband. You told him he loved that baby girl, but you were hungry. Something about you all having to obey the ruling class."

"You were ssspying on me?" Millie pointed a gloved finger at Alois and started to say something but belched with droopy eyes instead.

"You are in no condition to drive. Let me take you home." Alois tried to take the bottle of gin from Millie, but she snatched it out of her hand, sloshing gin all over her face just as camera flashes blinded them through the windows all around the vehicle.

Millie stumbled out of her car, her head wobbling. "What's—*hic*—the meaning of this?" she hiccupped, dropping her bottle, which rolled under the car tire. Her eyes blinked double-time, trying to focus.

"Mrs. Gurney called us to come here and film you, Lady Pimbledon—said it was imperative for your safety," said a younger member of the camera crew, while an older woman continued to film the conversation.

"Alois, you've been spying on me—*hic*—trying to, to set me up," said Millie. The upper button of her blouse finally came undone after hanging on by a thread.

"I did no such thing," said Alois, trying to pull Millie's scarf down over her exposed cleavage. "Ms. Johns sent me here to get some medicine for her stomach. Who exactly gave you all the message to come here?"

The crew exchanged sheepish glances.

"Ms. Johns told us all we know," said another member holding a long microphone.

While a woman from the film crew forced Millie into her car, Millie began mumbling scriptures: "The wicked spies upon the righteous and—*hic*—seeks to kill him. . . . Don't curse the king or the rich, or some winged creature will tell on you. . . . So, they watched him and sent spies, who—*hic*—pretended to be sincere, that they might catch him in something he said and deliver him to the authorities!"

"Mrs. Gurney, you didn't get permission to leave Therapon Hall," said the younger of the film crew. "You should come back with me, and someone else will return the car you stole."

"Stole?" yelled Alois. "Ms. Johns gave me her key to get her some medicine. Hold on; I want to see if what she said was true." Alois pulled free from the man's grip and made a dash into the drugstore. She quickly found the diarrhea medicine and took it to the nearest available counter.

"I need to charge this to Lady Pimbledon," said Alois.

"Sorry?" said the young girl behind the counter, shaking her head slightly.

"Lady Millie S. Pimbledon, the owner of Therapon Hall. All her servants charge items to her."

"Oh, now I know who you are referring to. But she has no account with us, and none of her servants have ever been in this store as far as I remember. Sorry."

The film crew came up to the counter and grabbed Alois.

"Let go of me," growled Alois. "See? Ms. Johns is a liar! The servants have never even been in this store."

"Security needed at terminal two," said the girl on the phone behind the register. Patrons throughout the store paused from their shopping and turned to face Alois.

"That won't be necessary. Lisa just made a mistake—came to the wrong store," said the older woman in the film crew. She tossed a ten-pound sterling on the counter, handed Alois the medicine, and pulled her out of the store.

"Wait. Why did you call me 'Lisa' in there?" asked Alois. "You don't want people to know who you are? Just what have you got to hide, huh?"

"Mrs. Gurney, they were calling for security because of your fit of paranoia back there. We were merely trying to protect you and the show's reputation. You have committed a major production violation. Now either cooperate with us, or we will report you to the producers."

When Alois returned to Therapon Hall with the diarrhea medicine, Ms. Johns came storming up to her.

"So, you're the thief who stole my car for your little publicity stunt. I hope you're happy, bringing shame on Lady Pimbledon as you did."

"You mean you weren't even sick? You—you set all of this up, not me!" hissed Alois, fighting the desire to pounce on the snake of a maid.

Ms. Johns shook her dust rag at Alois in the great hall. "Oh, I think the whole world is starting to see your family for what you are—a bunch of money-grubbing liars. Are the new reports true: 'You've never owned property in Wadebridge, England'?"

"The Gurney's don't have to justify ourselves to you or anyone. I should think the camera in my room caught you giving me your car keys, begging me to get your diarrhea medicine." Alois tossed the key and chalky blue medicine at Ms. John's feet.

"Actually, the film crew tried to get that footage, but somebody turned off the camera in our rooms, Mummy," said Presley, after rounding the corner from the servants' kitchen with his father. "They said you were filmed going into the control room before the camera was turned off, Ms. Johns."

"That is a bunch of codswallop. Besides, we have a cabinet full of stomach medicine," said Ms. Johns. "I can see why you need extra because you all are obviously full of it."

"You're th-the liar, Ms. J-Johns," stammered Levi. A thin stream of drool poured from his mouth, and he was visibly shaking, so Alois put her arm around him and helped him back to their room to avoid further questioning and possible humiliation for her husband.

Later that evening, Alois forced Levi to remain in bed and rest while she turned on the television. The Benefactrix reality show came on, and the entire day's events played out in digital color. Alois was horrified that the show didn't edit out her hanging upside down from the rope, her underwear shining in the sun. But she was glad the drone had captured video evidence of Ms. Johns, who clearly noticed Alois calling for help before she reluctantly decided to rescue Alois by letting her through the window.

"Well, there you have it, Ladies and Gentlemen. Did the maid, Ms. Johns, only help save Lady Gurney after the camera caught her trying to leave the Gurneys' bedroom? On your mobiles, vote three for 'Yes' and four for 'No,'" the host requested of the viewers with more of an expression of excitement than concern. After a commercial, the words "The Lady is a Thief?" rolled across the screen along with a recording of Ms. Johns running down the hall, accusing Alois of stealing her car keys and fleeing while she was in the lavatory.

"That lying bitch!" growled Alois, raising her arms in the air, jerking the bed, which startled Levi, who had just fallen asleep.

"She could've easily stolen her car. There is something phony about Mrs. Gurney," said the butler, Mr. Shaw, sitting in a chair in a private interview. "She holds her teacup with her pinky finger pointed and stirs her tea instead of gently folding. Even her son asked, and I quote, 'Can I git a glass of iced tea?' I mean, can you imagine such an abomination?"

The television panned to a snippet of Millie Pimbledon crawling out of her car, staggering drunk.

"Coming up next: speaking of surprise drinking habits, what about the stunning revelations concerning Lady Pimbledon? Is this a case of Lady Gurney outing someone else's drinking habits to distract from her own bourgeois style of taking tea?"

When the entire segment of Millie's drunkenness had

ended, the host looked directly into the camera.

"It seems when Millie S. Pimbledon returns from church every week, she isn't full of the spirit; she's drunk on spirits," said the host, folding his hands over his pink-striped jacket with an air of disappointment. "Was Lady Gurney really trying to help Lady Pimbledon or humiliate her? And, again, what about the maid—Ms. Johns? Is she a hero for rescuing Lady Gurney, as some say, or is she secretly trying to drive the Gurney family from Therapon Hall . . . one way or another? Stay tuned for the next episode to see how these new revelations unfold."

Alois turned off the television. She had hoped to see some footage of the car that tried to ram her off the road. Of course, not a camera in all of Northampton managed to capture that. And the directors or producers had edited out Alois going into the drug store, which would have proved that none of the servants ever shopped there. It had to be one of the servants who had tried to kill her, she imagined.

Why would any of the bigshots in the film crew try to harm one of their stars?

"Well, that's it; we're done for. Millie will never believe I didn't plan her humiliation, but Levi, I'll not allow you to go back up on the roof ever again. You can hardly even walk now. Were you able to eat anything this evening?"

After no response, Alois looked over at Levi. He was asleep. Again, she felt so alone. Her every action became twisted by the servants and the media. The entire world thought they knew her, but she had no one to confide in.

Was this what it felt like to be a celebrity? Surely Millie would kick them out on the street by sunrise.

CHAPTER TEN

Alois took control in the kitchen and blended some fruits and vegetables in a blender, hoping Levi could get some food down his throat. He managed to drink half the mixtures using a straw. Alois knew she wasn't going to be able to hide Levi's illness from her kids for much longer. Already Presley and Tara-Belle were staring at their father with long faces as he became shakier and skinnier each passing day. Presley's scissors overcut the obituary section from the stack of newspapers. This was his new assignment. According to the servants, Millie liked to read every obituary in England while having her breakfast.

"Mummy, Daddy, what is a snuff film?" asked Presley, unfolding one of the newspapers and holding it close to his face.

"No film that a proper young man should be watching," said Alois, pointing a carrot at Presley. "Snuff is tobacco, and it'll cause mouth cancer. Honestly, is this what they're showing to children these days?"

"But it says right here in this London newspaper that we are in one, Mummy. It says police have been called to investigate The Benefactrix show for tricking the Gurneys into starring in a snuff film. They must know Daddy used to chew snuff."

The servants became still and quiet. Levi scratched his forehead and grew paler.

"That gossip rag belongs in the rubbish," said Ms. Johns, grabbing for the newspaper, but Presley ducked under the kitchen table, gripping the paper for his life. He panted out his words now:

"A snuff film is an illegal movie where someone actually kills one of its cast members while filming it. It says these films have become more and more perverse these days."

"What does perverts mean, Mummy?" asked Tara-Belle.

Alois got chill bumps. Did the cameras somehow record what Alois had suspected about Millie being a baby-eating lizard humanoid? Was the Gurney family really in danger?

Levi coughed like he was choking. He grabbed his throat.

Mr. Shaw leaned over the backside of the table, snatched the newspaper out of Presley's hands, and wadded it into a ball.

"Levi, you are looking rather peckish. You really must see a doctor," said Mr. Shaw. "I'm sure The Benefactrix will thrive without you."

Ms. Johns nearly dropped her teacup. She looked over the top of eyeglasses at the butler as if he had just cursed out her mother.

"It's just a sore throat. Levi shouldn't have been up on

the roof in the chilly wind," snapped Alois, sloshing the remaining juice down the garbage disposal, trying to hold back tears. Levi had told her, not long after he was diagnosed with ALS, that when the time came and he could no longer eat, he did not want to be hooked up to a feeding tube. He made Alois promise that she wouldn't go against his wishes.

Ms. Johns hardly even looked at Alois or her family during the rest of breakfast. The meddling old maid knew too much about the Gurneys. She had to have been snooping through Alois's and Levi's things. Alois froze while washing her plate and silverware. Oh goodness, she wondered: did Ms. Johns find her Mississippi driver's license or welfare card she had left in her purse? Alois nearly dropped the plate she was now drying with an old towel embroidered with a likeness of Therapon Hall. All the Gurneys could do at this point was keep working and hope Millie would see the truth. Alois felt kinda bad at times, hoping Millie wouldn't hold out much longer with her liver disease—especially with Levi racing toward death's door himself.

Mr. Shaw looked at his daily schedule and cleared his throat. "You should be glad to know, Mrs. Gurney, that Lady Pimbledon has scheduled a historical re-enactment for today, which means no roof work in the chilly air," he said mockingly. "However, this means that guests will be touring Therapon Hall throughout the day, and we must all look our best and be on cue."

"What do we have to do—dust the hornets' nests?"

asked Presley.

Mr. Shaw looked down his bulbous nose at the Gurneys. "Presley, you will be here in the kitchen, helping Ms. Johns prepare finger sandwiches for the guests."

"Fingers?" Presley's chin shriveled, and his eyebrows scrunched as he looked up at Alois. "They eat fingers here?"

Alois pinched Presley hard on the back of his arm to get him to shut up. Not only did he accidentally voice the R in "fingers," he made it look obvious that the Gurneys weren't from England. Of course, she couldn't be too hard on the boy; the only sandwiches Presley had ever eaten were mayonnaise sandwiches, and if the Gurneys were lucky, they might get a slice of canned organ meat between the bread.

"Ears," said Presley, the way Suki had taught him. "Sounds awfully delicious, really." He gulped and forced a disturbing grin.

"Will Lady Pimbledon be requiring us to baptize the sandwich meats?" asked Taylan.

"No, only the venison she's having for lunch. She's doesn't care for sandwiches," said the butler.

"Good, because I don't have time to make any runs for more holy water," said the maid.

"Mummy can cast the devil out of the fingers if you'd like. She put me on the straight and narrow," said Presley, causing Alois's chest to sink with embarrassment.

Mr. Shaw sighed before continuing: "Mr. Gurney, you will serve as the footman and greet all the guests at the door. And, Mrs. Gurney, you and Taylan will take the guests on a tour of the entire estate. Tara-Belle will remain with her tutor, safely out of everyone's hair. And I will be working the gates, selling tickets. If Lady Pimbledon feels up to making an appearance to her guests, you are to keep out of the way and do not interrupt her. After the humiliation you caused her, Mrs. Gurney, it is crucial that she make a good impression on the guests and media."

Alois stood up and smashed her teacup on the kitchen floor. "You all set me up. You knew Lady Pimbledon would be at the chemist, drinking. That's why you sent me there. Then you sent the film crew, making it look like I tipped them off about her. But what I want to know is which one of you tried to kill me on the road to the chemist?"

Levi, Presley, and Tara-Belle jerked their heads toward Alois. She had desperately intended to keep this from her family but didn't want the world to believe lies about her either.

"Kill you?" said Taylan, choking on his toast and jam.

"Ah, see? There she goes again," said Ms. Johns, wiping the splattered tea off her white apron with a dishcloth. "Making more baseless accusations because she knows the cameras are filming her. Now excuse me while I go air out Lady Pimbledon's late-spring gowns."

Mr. Shaw snatched the bottom of his tuxedo down over his waist as if Alois had caused his jacket to wrinkle like his face.

"We don't have time for any more games, Mrs.

Gurney," he said in his sternest tone. "Your historical uniforms have been delivered to your rooms. You all have half an hour to change and proceed to your posts before the guests start arriving. Understand?"

Everyone nodded and headed to their rooms to change into uniform. Alois's attire was about the same, except for the extra lace ruffles on the white apron. The black dress underneath was longer than her standard uniform, and she had a white-ruffled hat that secured at the back of her head. Levi came back from the lavatory looking more handsome than Alois had ever seen. His footman uniform was a black tuxedo, but he was holding a long white strip of fabric with one hand, and his other hand was pressing hard against his belly.

"Are you sick? Is your stomach hurting?" whispered Alois, hoping the camera wouldn't record their conversation.

"No," whispered Levi. "Ca-can't fa-fasten buttons." He removed his trembling hand, and his black vest was completely unfastened, so she began hooking the buttons as fast as she could.

"Wh-what is . . . what is this for?" whispered Levi, holding up the strip of fabric.

"I don't know—a belt, you think?" Alois examined it for a minute, then noticed Levi was missing a bowtie. He had never worn a necktie in his entire life, especially a bowtie. "I think it goes around your neck." She wrapped the fabric around his neck and tied it like she did her shoestrings. It looked awful.

Levi stood as tall as he could in front of the wall mirror. "Look's good ta—to m-me." He tried to swallow but drool poured from his mouth. And for the first time in Alois's life, she watched her grown husband let out a gut-wrenching, ugly-faced cry. The doctors had warned her that the ALS disease would eventually make Levi uncontrollably emotional.

How did she ever think this plan of coming to England would work? She got one of Levi's handkerchiefs and cleaned up his face. She couldn't bring herself to tell Levi that she didn't know how to tie a bowtie. And in his slow condition, they had better get a head start to their assigned posts. She was now clutching her stomach as they inched toward the great hall.

Mr. Shaw took one look at Levi's makeshift bowtie and his entire face crumpled into a frown. "Mr. Gurney!" he snorted, before Alois jerked him away and near a partition of velvet ropes, which the servants had put in place to keep guests from getting too close to the priceless antiques.

"If you dare fuss at my husband, I swear I'll take those tails on your coat and hang you from the chandelier. Levi—he's a little upset right now. He—he injured his hand on the roof and can't tie his bowtie. He looks just fine, and that's that!"

Mr. Shaw's face swelled until tiny red veins appeared on his eyeballs. He snatched up a cardboard box of pink tour tickets from the hall table and marched out of the old estate. Ms. Johns grabbed Levi's shoulders and shoved him beside the front door.

"Levi, you will open the door and take the tickets from the guests. . . . Watch the grandfather clock, and every hour, direct whatever guests that have arrived into the library where Alois will begin the tour of the main lower rooms. I will take over the tour on the grand staircase. Have I made myself clear?" asked Ms. Johns. Over the tops of her eyeglasses, her gaze settled on Levi's bowtie as if she were seeing her own house go up in flames.

"Ears!" Alois blurted. "I do believe you've said enough."

The pale mole on Ms. Johns's left jaw twitched. She handed Alois a corsage of pink roses she had been holding. "I have to check on that boy of yours in the kitchen. Take this to Millie in her room. She wants to wear it on her dress," the maid said before stomping past Alois toward the kitchen.

Alois made her way to Millie's room, and before her knuckles tapped against the door, she heard Millie sobbing. She eased the door open. Millie had her back to the door, talking to a framed photo of her husband on a dresser lit by candles.

"Wilfred, please forgive me. I know Mary was your baby girl. I wasn't jealous. I only wanted what was best for our niece and us. If I could've had children, I would have—it was those corsets proper ladies were expected to wear."

Alois's ears burned from this confession. Mary was Levi's mother, who Lady Pimbledon claimed went missing as soon as Millie's sister disinherited Mary.

Millie placed a plate of brown cookies underneath Wilfred's photo.

"Here, I brought your favorite biscuits—bourbon cream—for your birthday. I only nibbled a bit on the corners. Oh, Wilfred, I didn't drive Mary away from Northampton. If I had known you would kill yourself, I would never have pressured Mary into marrying Charles. The girl turned on us because we had her best interest in mind—that little ingrate! Now I admit it's my fault for overspending and forcing you to let me throw all of those lavish parties. You see, Wilfred, Charles was a wealthy English lord, and we were starving because of all my spending. He promised to fund improvements for Therapon Hall if Mary agreed to marry him. And she would've married Lord Charles if that American preacher hadn't convinced her that we were nothing but worldly and wicked Brits. Which is exactly what Levi said his mother called us after they first arrived at Therapon Hall. Oh, Wilfred, I'm convinced Mary didn't marry some unknown lord; she married that horrid American preacher."

Millie opened the lid on a jewelry box on the dresser and removed a necklace. Diamonds, Alois imagined.

"That man even made Mary stop wearing the heirloom jewelry we gave her. He convinced her she looked like a teenage Jezebel."

Alois collapsed against the doorframe. She felt like a hot knife had sliced deep into her chest and stomach. To think, she had wanted to kill Millie earlier, when it was all a gross misunderstanding. Alois's heart pumped faster. She had to stop calling her dangerous stupidity "misunderstandings." She should've remembered enough from history—how the ruling class of England always wanted their children to marry other aristocrats. Maybe the ruling class weren't no lizard people despite what her hometown had been swearing. Maybe simple folks like Alois keep reinventing those theories, hoping to prove their lack of education was somehow smarter than the elite.

Alois stroked her chin. Levi's mother, Mary, must have really been a real rebel to choose a poor Pentecostal preacher from the United States to wed instead of an English lord. So much of a rebel that her uncle, Wilfred, killed himself, and her mother died after cutting her off financially.

Thirty minutes later, feeling far less headstrong, Alois returned to her post in the library just as the first group of tourists arrived at the door.

Levi's hand trembled as he struggled to turn the old brass knob and pull open the massive wooden door. Alois resisted running to help Levi. She waited just inside the library entry and kept peeping into the hall, checking on her husband.

"Wuh—wel—to Thera—Hall," Levi struggled to welcome the group of about forty people. He held out a wicker basket for the guests to deposit their tickets. The guests scooted in close and turned their heads in every direction, trying to take in the beauty of the hall all at once.

"Hey, look, guys, it's Gurney, it's Gurney," said a heavyset man with a short dark beard, before slapping Levi on the arm. "Man, I hafta say: when you all first arrived on the show, I never thought you'd end up scrubbing toilets for old Millie. Ha-ha! Come on now, shoot straight with us; where are you guys really from, huh?"

Levi's lips tightened, and his chin spasmed, so he looked down at the tickets in the basket.

"Can Presley sign our brochures?" asked a red-headed girl squeezing in front of five other girls who were standing on tiptoes, searching around the hall for him.

Levi struggled to answer all their questions, but luckily, everyone hushed their chatter and became distracted when Millie S. Pimbledon came teetering down the great hall in a black beaded gown and a diamond tiara. She had clipped more live butterflies in her hair—dull blue ones this time.

"I'm so frightfully glad you all could attend my historical re-enactment," said Millie, as the film crew surrounded her with cameras and microphones. "As I'm sure you all know, I am Lady Pimbledon. In its heyday, Therapon Hall was maintained by over one hundred servants. This grand manor house was host to members of the royal family and once held the grand honor of—"

"Excuse me," said a tall man with gelled-back wavy hair. He stepped forward in front of the cameras. "Tom Gordon here with Northampton's own Cinema Singular Productions. Guests, do not be fooled by what you all see here. It's time the world knows the truth. I have uncovered something that will expose The Benefactrix reality show as a massive fraud."

"Cut!" Derick Hoosier ordered the film crew to stop recording, but a few of the tourists held up their phones to capture the event.

"That's right; keep recording," said Tom Gordon. "My company will pay you for any video evidence you can provide us."

A few people gasped and stepped back when Levi dropped the basket of tickets and collapsed on the floor. Alois shoved her way through the crowd to get to her husband. He was soon able to sit up, though he had hit his head on the floor, leaving a red bump on his forehead.

"Are you okay, Levi?" asked Alois, while Presley came running from the kitchen, dropping a silver tray of finger sandwiches. The girls who had been looking for Presley squealed with brightened faces, and they handed him their brochures to sign. He took them but turned to see if his father was okay before autographing the pamphlets.

"I'm all right. But it's time we te—we tell the truth," stammered Levi.

"The truth of what?" asked Millie, stroking her neck with her ringed fingers. "I demand to know what is going on here."

Alois knew Levi was right; they had been found out. And with Levi's declining health, they couldn't keep fulfilling their contract on the show. With Presley on one side of her and Levi under her other arm, Alois decided to talk in her normal accent and reveal who they really were.

"What Mr. Gordon said is true, I'm afraid," said Alois, to the sounds of shock. "We are the Gurney family, but we ain't got no fancy titles. We ain't got no mansion either—well, we had us a home until it got condemned by our uppity neighbors. We're from Wadebridge, Mississippi, and we ain't never set foot in England until we agreed to be on this-here show."

"Ah-ha!" yelled Ms. Johns, after entering the hall with Taylan to sweep up the spilled sandwiches. With a smirk, she strutted straight up to Alois. "That explains the nasal drawl that occasionally slips through those lying Yankee lips of yours."

Two of the girls still waiting for Presley to autograph their brochures, crinkled the pamphlets in their hands, then backed away from him with embarrassed grimaces.

"That is indeed a shocking revelation, Mrs. Gurney," said Tom. "But the fraud I was referring to is Millie S. Pimbledon."

"That is bollocks! Don't you dare speak of Lady Pimbledon that way," shouted Taylan, with a mouthful of spoiled sandwiches, spewing crumbs over his tuxedo.

"The Gurneys are the frauds!" added Ms. Johns. "I saw Alois's driver's license and her welfare card. I took a picture of them on my mobile."

"I'm sure this is all just a misunderstanding," said Derick Hosier, the producer. He had turned pale and ignored the director, who was waiting for permission to resume filming. "Cinema Singular is our main competitor in the U.K. I will not stand for this—you sneaking in on our production and spreading lies, trying to destroy our ratings."

The second round of tourists gathered on the steps outside, pounding on the door. Derick's assistant, Suki, ran to the entrance and leaned against the door with all her strength.

"Is this the sort of sham your company puts out these days, Hosier? You see, Millie here is not dying of anything except from lack of attention, perhaps." Tom held up a copy of her medical records. "In fact, she has lost her entire fortune except for her three homeless servants, who remain loyal to her and her crumbling estate. And it's obvious she has tricked the Gurney family into becoming her servants just as she tricked many other servants over the years—making them think they will eventually get paid some grand inheritance. Who gave you the green light to produce The Benefactrix, Hosier—some underground human trafficking ring?"

"I knew it," shouted a woman from the crowd. "What lord or lady scrubs floors and repairs someone else's roof? They've done something to the Gurney family—turned them into zombies. Look at Mr. Gurney; he's hardly recognizable now."

Alois and Presley lifted Levi off the floor and maneuvered him through the tourists and further down the candlelit hall, where they lowered him onto a sofa with gold-leaf carvings. Presley ran to the kitchen to get a cold rag for his father's head injury.

Presley pulled something wrapped in a napkin from his

coat pocket. "Here, Daddy; I saved you a sandwich. It's doesn't really have any fingers in it." He held it out for Levi, who shook his head with distant eyes.

"It's no use, Presley. He can't eat," said Alois, and the reality of this had finally gripped her.

"But why?" asked Presley, before distant yelling distracted them.

"We demand you unblock the door and let us out. You can't keep us in here," said one of the tourists, while others gasped.

"Where's my mobile? I'm calling the cops, I am," said a woman, fishing a cell phone from her purse. Her hands shook so hard she dropped the phone on her foot.

With sweat misting her face, Suki reluctantly moved away from the rattling door, and when it finally opened, the incoming tourists collided into the fleeing crowd.

"For God's sake, people, don't come in," cried a woman, barreling through the crowd. "It's not a re-enactment. It's a trap!"

"They tried to lock us in here. They'll turn you into slaves," panted a middle-aged man, holding his grandchildren's hands, dragging them past the slower-moving tourists.

"Somebody go get help," said another woman, turning around to leave.

As Alois watched the dwindling commotion, she got a vision of her family stranded on a tiny island with nothing but a single palm tree for security.

"What's gonna happen now?" asked Presley. His chest

heaved under his coat while Derick and Tom rolled around the hall floor, wrestling and hitting each other before the film crew separated them. The servants cornered Millie, and they soon got into a shouting match before Millie slapped Ms. Johns across her face, knocking her eyeglasses askew.

"Help me get Levi to his bed," Alois said to Presley. "Then I want us to find Tara-Belle. You two are sleeping in our room tonight. I don't want you out of my sight."

Presley agreed, and they headed toward the back stairs before Alois paused.

"You know what? Screw this!" she said, turning to her left and grabbing the carved post at the end of the handrail. "This might be our last day in the house, and I don't care what anyone thinks; we're taking the grand stairs."

"All right!" said Presley, helping heave his father up the first step.

CHAPTER ELEVEN

Alois watched through the bedroom window as police and the world press surrounded the estate. Even helicopters and vehicles belonging to American news networks squeezed between local news sources.

"Is the door locked?" asked Alois?

"Yes, Mummy. You've asked me that three times," said Presley, sitting on the edge of the bed while his father slept two feet away from him.

"You can drop the English accent, Son. It's no use being anything other than ourselves," sighed Alois. "The cameras have already recorded everything the world needs to see."

"I hate this place," huffed Presley. He grabbed a pillow from the bed and, jumping as high as he could, knocked the video camera off the wall above his head. The camera landed on the floor, and he stomped it until it broke into three pieces. Presley and Tara-Belle ran to their mother's side when a loud banging rattled the door.

"Police! Open the door," a man's deep voice ordered.

"Are they gonna shoot us, Maw?" asked Presley, as the banging continued, waking Levi.

"Probably not here," said Alois. She removed her arms from around her children and inched toward the door before unlocking it.

A bulky police officer flashed his badge at Alois. Just behind the man stood all three of Millie's servants with frowns locked on their faces. The butler, Mr. Shaw, seemed to be biting his lower lip, and his face was paler and eyes vacant.

"Sorry to bother you, Mrs. Gurney, but I need to ask you and your family a few questions," said the officer.

"Alois, dear," purred the maid, Ms. Johns, gliding past the officer to brace her hands on Alois's shoulders, followed by Mr. Shaw, who sat on the bed beside Levi and placed his hand on his upper back. With a concerned expression, Taylan, the gardener, knelt in front of Presley and Tara-Belle, who huddled beside the wardrobe.

"We know you must be relieved this awful ordeal is over. We're all free," continued Ms. Johns.

Alois backed away from the maid. "What do you mean by 'We're all free'?"

"Oh, the poor dear has been through so much trauma she's delusional," Ms. Johns said to the police officer before embracing Alois again. "Mr. Shaw, Taylan, and I owe you and your family a huge apology. When you first arrived at Therapon Hall, we were envious of your titles. American or not, we had no idea you were just like us— mere commoners trapped here—just trying to survive."

"Trying to survive you and all your devil tricks," spat Alois. "Ha! I didn't see none of you climbing up on the roof."

"That was Millie's orders, not ours," said Ms. Johns. "We're free from her now. We're no longer her slaves. You all think you've had it rough. Every day I had to prepare her baths of sparkling water and rub lotion in all her crannies besides all the other things I had to do for her."

"The re-enactment is over, woman. You can stop whatever this performance is you're giving," said Alois. "The Gurney family ain't nobody's slaves. We chose to help out around here. We . . . like it."

"That's not true," said Ms. Johns, before turning her head toward the officer. "The Gurney's are obviously afraid of Millie's cruel punishments. But we have a chance, Mrs. Gurney—you, me, all of us—a chance to make Millie pay us what we deserve in court. All we need you to do is confess the truth."

Alois threw her arms up with a groan. "I already told you the truth. We like it here, and we want to help Millie out any way we can."

"The woman can't be helped. I've tried for over fifty years. She never comes through with a promise," said Mr. Shaw, looking feverish now.

"You told me you've only worked for Millie for twenty years," said Alois.

"I meant twenty, of course," said Mr. Shaw. "After the abuse and everything we have been through, it's remarkable that I even know my name."

"Oh, yes, lots of abuse." Taylan nodded furiously. He reached up from his kneeling position and gently grabbed

Tara-Belle's wrists. "Tell the nice police officer the truth," said Taylan. "Tell him how you almost died from falling off the ladder."

"I cwimbed the ladder. It was fun," giggled Tara-Belle. "But Mummy says I not posed to do it no more."

"Well, how about you, Presley? Tell him how you almost died—you know—from Millie forcing you to climb that tree with the hornets' nest and all."

Presley looked at his mother as if for approval, then with a shrug, he shook his head. Taylan stood up and grabbed Presley's face between his hands. Taylan then forced his face toward Levi, who was sitting on the edge of the bed, drooling.

"Look at him, chap—your own father. Your mum said so herself—said he was in this shape because he injured himself from Millie making him work on the roof."

Alois couldn't look her son in the eyes. She had used working on the roof as an excuse for Levi's illness to avoid the truth of his condition. But she had promised not to break her vow of secrecy with Levi.

Presley's eyes became moist, and his lids lowered. He knocked Taylan's hands off his face.

"My paw is just sick, that's all. He'll be okay soon. We weren't no slaves. We were just fixing up our house we're supposed to get."

Taylan lifted his hands in a hopeless gesture. His eyebrows joined in a frown. "Millie had me thinking I would inherit her estate. 'You keep improving my gardens, Taylan Chowdhury, and all of this might be yours,'" she said to me. "I even cut my hair and stopped wearing turbans for Her Ladyship. I was hoping to find my family and move them here from India."

"Don't you all get it?" asked Mr. Shaw, standing to his feet. "That's the same story Lady Pimbledon—Millie— led all of us to believe. Year after year, we have slaved here for free, believing that that vile woman's fortune—this estate—would someday be our reward."

Levi looked up at Mr. Shaw and then at the police officer. He tried to swallow. "*Ugh*, we . . . not slaves." He shoved a trembling finger at the two men.

"That will be all," said the officer. "I'm afraid there isn't enough evidence to support your claims, Ms. Johns, Mr. Shaw. . . ."

"Not enough evidence?" hissed the maid. "Millie is a tyrant. Her husband lived in fear of her as well. The poor man committed suicide on a Sunday because he couldn't deal with her anymore, especially when she's drunk. The whole world saw her in one of her drunken states, and I finally had a camera crew at my disposal to catch her at the chemist."

"There we go! I'm glad you finally admitted to sending the film crew to the drug store," said Alois, shaking her hands frustratedly at the maid. "You accused me of stealing your car to hurt poor Lady Pimbledon's reputation."

"You have your own car?" the officer asked Ms. Johns. He re-examined the records in his hands as if he had missed something.

After an awkward pause, Ms. Johns replied, "Yes, but it's actually one of Millie's that I use to go to market and other errands—for her, of course."

"You, an alleged victim of human trafficking—an alleged house-bound slave—you have access to a car, and you never tried to escape or go for help while out on one of your shopping errands?" asked the officer, taking more notes with his pen.

Ms. Johns turned red-faced, and her chest puffed under her tight uniform. "Yes, but Lady Pimbledon, she, uh— she threatened to have us hunted down and thrown from the Tower of London if we tried to escape. Women like her have money and powerful connections—at least we thought she did."

The officer's face tightened in a slight frown. "So, which is it with you all? A: You continued working here with no pay, hoping for a reward of Millie's fortune and estate? Or B: You wanted to escape but feared for your lives?"

Ms. Johns placed her fingertips on her chin and searched the other two servants' faces as though looking for backup.

"Um, it was more like 'A' at first," said Taylan. "But then we started fearing for our lives, right? I've read some scary history about members of the aristocracy with all their connections to the Crown. If you went against Her Majesty's pleasure, you'd be drawn and quartered."

"Alright, I'll make a report," sighed the officer. "But you'll have to take the matter up with a solicitor. Our job here is done. Sorry to bother you, Mr. and Mrs. Gurney."

The officer tipped his hat to Alois and Levi before leaving their bedroom. On the way out the door, Ms. Johns turned back around and flashed a murderous glance at the Gurney family. Alois might have fallen for the servants' story if they hadn't been so cruel to her family—if they hadn't been caught lying to them.

Later that night, Presley and Tara-Belle slept on the floor while Alois tossed and turned. Her thoughts jumbled in her head. What would happen to her family now? They couldn't afford any lawsuits from the production company. Her thoughts were interrupted when she kept hearing strange knocking noises and scratches.

"Stop making that noise," Alois fussed at her kids. She leaned over the bed, and they were sound asleep with a nest of clutter around—as much as they could gather in such a neat house: dirty clothes, bits of paper, and even a crystal vase they had taken off the dresser. God! Did this mess bring them comfort? Did they miss living in chaos? Clutter comfort was entirely her and Levi's fault for being so lazy—for surrendering to defeat and raising their kids in a dump of a house back in Mississippi. So help her God; if they had to go back to some tiny shack again, she would at least keep it as clean and neat as possible. Her children deserved better—they deserved some sort of future.

Her dog's barking and howling echoed up the attic floor of the giant estate. Then Alois heard a loud yelp. Had something happened to Egghead? She tiptoed out of bed and crept toward the window overlooking the formal gardens. Her breath fogged the glass before she saw Taylan under the moonlight, chopping down the hedges. It appeared as though he had taken an army tank and had trampled down the flowerbeds and knocked over all the marble statues, as well.

Alois heard another series of noises echoing up the hall. She sneaked out of the bedroom, eased down the grand staircase, and peeped between the carved posts under the handrailing. Mr. Shaw was headed toward the front open door, pushing the antique grandfather clock on a four-wheeled dolly, while Ms. Johns carried a laundry basket full of silver from the dining room. On her head was Millie's tiara, and around her neck, she had stacked at least ten or twelve jeweled necklaces.

Alois's blood heated. She realized yet another strange commonality with Millie now, for they had both had their property demolished and stolen from them. She wanted to yell at the servants to stop, and she would if her husband was healthy enough to help defend her and if she didn't have her kids in the same house with these thieves. This ballsy act was dangerous and daring. Who knows what harm they might be capable of doing if she tried to intervene?

She got to worrying about her kids and Levi, so Alois sneaked back to her bedroom and locked the door, unintentionally waking Presley and Tara-Belle.

"Is somethin' wrong, Maw?" Presley looked over at Levi sleeping. Then he rubbed his eyes while his grown-out hair was sticking up like some of the wild kids she had seen at the airport when they first arrived in England.

Alois whispered everything she had just seen happen. " . . . I dunno. Surely the servants will be outta here by morning."

"You don't think they did anything to Ms. Millie, did they?" asked Presley.

"I dunno that either," whispered Alois, while her daughter crawled in her lap and clung to her. "But just in case, I don't want y'all going anywhere without me, understand?"

"Emm, I left my doll in the liberry. They gonna taked her," said Tara-Belle, her eyes elongated pitifully as she stretched her little arms toward the door.

"I don't think the servants will go in the library. Your doll will still be there in the morning. Don't you go a-gittin' too big for your britches and go looking for it, young lady," said Alois, gently patting Tara on her back. "We need to learn to take care of what we got. As long as we have each other, we don't need no stuff—don't need a thing."

The truth was Alois didn't know what to expect, but she mustn't scare her kids any more than they already were. She was going to have to be the only caretaker of her kids from now on.

CHAPTER TWELVE

By morning, Alois and her kids left Levi in the bed as they began roaming through the quiet estate. Everywhere they looked down the halls, all the doors leading into bedrooms, studies, and drawing rooms had been left open. Old paintings were missing, and antique furniture had been removed everywhere. On the back staircase, Alois stepped over a pile of lace doilies and a shattered wooden clock that used to chime a beautiful tune every hour when it sat on a fireplace mantel in the top-floor sitting room. The old wallpaper along the staircase wall had a deep rip that traveled for at least twelve horrifying feet. Alois shuddered. On the first-floor landing, someone had shoved a fireplace poker into a portrait of Millie—right through her painted thin lips.

"Maw, look!" panted Presley, pointing down the great hall to what appeared to be a dead woman in a lavender sleeping gown. The brassy helmet of hair gave the woman's identity away before Alois, Presley, and Tara-Belle came to a stop beside her twisted body. It was Millie, and she was clutching her tattered white debutante dress in her stiff hands—the dress she had worn when she had been presented before Queen Elizabeth II's Court.

Alois dropped to her knees and braced her right hand on Millie's arm. "Oh, bless yo' little old heart, Lady Pimbledon. I . . . I'm so sorry." Alois looked up at her children. "Presley and Tara, put your hands over your hearts and pay your respects."

"But, Maw," said Presley, with a scrunched forehead. "That's for the Pledge of Allegiance."

Alois's teeth jutted, and she thought her eyeballs would burst. "I don't care—you're gonna show this-here woman some respect." She snapped her fingers at them.

Presley and Tara-Belle placed their hands over their heats before the camera crew showed up outside, filming the destruction. When their cameras lowered toward Millie's body, still sprawled out near the open front door, they put down their cameras, took off their hats, and lowered their heads.

"Oh, my! This is awful. What happened?" asked the director.

"I'm not sure," said Alois. "The servants went nuts, took the furniture, and left sometime earlier this morning; I think."

"They'll pay for this. We need any evidence we can scrounge. Check the stationary cameras," the director ordered a girl from production. Immediately, she went running down the hall, jumping over abandoned cabinet drawers and a fancy brass candle holder.

Tara-Belles came bouncing out of the library with a big smile on her face. She had recovered her princess doll.

Alois realized the doll Suki gave her was as close as her baby girl would now ever get to feeling like a princess.

The girl from productions re-entered the hall with wild eyes and a crushed computer screen in her arms. "Someone demolished the camera control room! All the video evidence is gone," she said.

A moan coming from the floor at Alois's feet startled her. Millie had moved her arms.

"Maw! Mrs. Millie's done gone and resurrected," gasped Presley, stepping back several feet with a look of fright distorting his face.

"She wasn't dead—just drunk," said the director, helping Millie to her feet. Dried drool coated the edges of Millie's mouth like a glazed donut. Her eyeglasses had embedded into the top of her teased hair.

"Those ingrates took everything I had. I—I tried to stop them." Millie looked down at her tattered white dress, and her chin quivered. "What will I ever do?"

"Oh, quit your bellyaching, Lady Pimbledon! You still got two hands and two feet," said Alois, grabbing Millie's hands and raising them to her pitiful face. "You still have a mighty fine house. We're fixin' to clean this-here place up again." Alois snapped her fingers at her children. "Kids, get ta fixin'."

"Aw, Maw. Do we gotta?" whined Presley, looking around like a mouse in an open field.

"Did I mumble, boy? Remember, we're gonna start taking care of what we do have," said Alois. She bent over and began picking up dropped debris and broken knickknacks while her children began doing the same.

An hour or so later, Alois began cleaning up the emptied dining room. The servants didn't bother taking the dining table or the china cabinet, probably due to their enormous sizes. Alois swept up the smaller pieces of a shattered china serving bowl when Presley came running through the doorway.

"Paw got outta bed, Maw! He's climbed the ladder—said he was gonna help us fix the place up."

Alois felt a bilious pain knot up in the middle of her stomach. "Has Levi lost his mind? Tell 'im to git down offa that ladder this minute. I'm right behind you," Alois huffed as she ran behind Presley.

When she weaved through the scattered and squashed hedges that once were the formal gardens in front of the estate, she looked up and had another attack of the dizzies. Levi was nearly at the top of the ladder, carrying a basket of replacement slates on his shoulder.

"Paw, come down from yonder!" shouted Presley, waving his arms while Tara-Belle did the same.

"Levi Waylon Gurney, git down from there right now, ya hear me?" yelled Alois, pacing in circles in the shadow of a cameraman. "You ain't in no condition to be climbing ladders." She placed her hand over her eyebrows to block out the morning sun. "Oh, sweet baby Jaysus," she prayed that she was seeing things: A dark blob of what had to be her husband began plummeting to the ground. The nerve-wrenching sound of Presley's screaming shattered all hopes that Alois's eyesight had fooled her.

The closer she ran toward the fallen ladder, tears began to sting her eyes. She fell to the ground beside Levi, who lay face down.

"Call an ambulance. My husband has been hurt," Alois pleaded with the cameraman before he pulled out his cell phone and called for help.

"Git up, Daddy," begged Tara-Belle, pulling on the leg of his pants.

"Levi, can you hear me?" asked Alois, trying to find a way to ease his pain, but she knew she had better not try to move him in case he injured his spine. A low groan escaped Levi's lips.

"Maw, Maw," stammered Presley, wiping a tear on his sleeve, before pointing at the wooden rung near the top of the ladder.

"What, Son, what?" asked Alois in an angry tone.

"Look closer, Maw. Somebody cut through this step in the ladder. And you can see some saw marks on the step above it. That's why Paw fell."

"It had to be Taylan. I caught him sawing down everything in the garden last night," said Alois, never dreaming that Taylan would go this far. Alois knew she should tell Presley and Tara-Belle about their father's terminal illness, but she couldn't bring herself to upset them more.

A half-hour later, Alois and Presley fidgeted in their seats in the emergency area of the hospital waiting room. Alois had left Tara-Belle with her tutor, hoping not to traumatize her any more than she already was. Her fingernail had scratched a hole in the fabric of the armrest of her chair. Through the door came Millie Pimbledon, and behind her, Derick Hoosier and his assistant, Suki, followed lastly by a couple from the filming crew, focusing their camera lenses on Millie as she stood like the queen and looked down at Alois.

"I want you to know that I feel simply awful about Levi's accident," said Millie. "How is the poor man?"

"Accident?" hissed Alois, slapping her hands on the chair arms, ready to lunge at Millie, but she forced herself to sit back down, especially with a camera in her face. "Taylan did this. He tampered with the ladder, knowing Levi had been working on the roof. We tried to tell you your servants were trying to get rid of us no matter what it took. But oh no, no, no; you just kept your little nose in the air and ignored us!"

"Now, let's all just calm down, Mrs. Gurney," said Derick. "I'm sure everything will turn out—"

"Excuse me," said a short woman with curly dark hair. She squeezed around Derick, Millie, and Suki, clutching a clipboard against her white lab coat. It was the doctor, and Alois could tell by her somber expression that Levi had died.

" . . . I'm afraid there was nothing we could do," said the doctor, grabbing Alois's hand as she and Presley began to sob.

"I shoulda kept beating Taylan when I had him down. I hate 'im. I hate 'im," sobbed Presley.

Millie cleared her throat, placed her gloved hands in

her lap, and smiled. "At my funeral, I want twelve English virgins to dance somberly on either side of my coffin." She lifted a finger, and her face hardened. "Now, it's important that I have an even number of girls and not too pretty, mind you."

While Suki tried to comfort Presley, the doctor squatted down in front of Alois. "Levi remained mostly unresponsive but right before his vital signs stopped, I believe I heard him say—oh never mind," said the doctor, standing upright. "I'm sure it was nothing."

"He spoke?" asked Alois, raising her head, still wishing she could have been by his side. "What was it? What did you hear?"

The doctor's full lips shifted to the side as if in doubt. "Well, I thought I heard him say, 'I wanted it this way.'"

After the doctor turned to leave, Derick and Millie both turned ashen in the face. Alois jumped up from her chair and started pacing around the room with her hands over her eyes. How could things get any worse? She couldn't even say goodbye to her husband.

Derick motioned for the male camera operator to move his camera from the doctor, who was now exiting the waiting room, to Alois. Realizing Derick was exploiting her husband's death and family's grief, she charged at Derick and punched him in the nose.

"This is your fault, too," growled Alois. "You knew the servants were targeting us, and you did nothing—just kept on filming. I want out of the contract. Me and my kids are done with your show."

Covering his bloody nose with his right hand, Derick blocked the camera lens with his other hand.

"Look, Mrs. Gurney, I know—I know how difficult this must be for you. It's tragic—it is," groaned Derick, bending over with two frightened eyes that seemed to plead with her. "You're free to back out of the contract if you feel that's your only choice. But just know that'll give me no other option except to sue you for breaking your contract. And trust me, that's the last thing I want to do, Mrs. Gurney—the last thing."

"*Humh*! Go ahead and sue us," shouted Alois, grabbing Presley's arm and pulling him out of his seat so they could leave. "We ain't got a nickel to our name. You and your greedy little lawyers will take that, too, you—goddamn disgusting piece of shit!" She pointed a finger at the cowering cameraman. "That there that I just said is what ya shoulda recorded for your stinkin' show."

Alois felt as though she had landed at the bottom of a ten-mile-deep septic tank. She had no clue how she would even get back home, much less pay for Levi's funeral. She couldn't believe becoming a hooker crossed her mind. Alois realized she must be stressed as she stomped out of the hospital with her son. What man would pay for a piece of her unless he was as hard up as she was? Forget the red-light district; she would have to work in the darkest corners of the broken-light district.

When she reached the glass doors to the hospital, she broke into tears and threw herself against the metal doorframe. The reality that Levi was gone hit her.

Somewhere deep in the maze of sterile halls, he took his last breath without her. Alois just knew if she took one step out the door, she'd somehow feel like she was abandoning him. But if she stayed, they might try to bill her for everything. And what would they do if she couldn't pay? Alois, again, got another vision of herself behind prison bars.

"Don't cry, Maw. I'll take care of you and Tara-Belle," whispered Presley, taking his mother's hand.

CHAPTER THIRTEEN

Alois began to panic as she and Presley walked fast down
the long road outside the hospital. Trees on one side and
fresh-cut grass on the other. When they finally reached the
main street, it was late afternoon, and Alois's feet were
hurting.

"But, Maw, where are we going? I'm hungry," whined
Presley. He paused and looked at the pub on the corner.

"We can't do anything until we get Tara-Belle." Alois
looked down both ends of the street, trying to remember
the direction the ambulance had taken to the hospital.

"You mean we hafta walk back to Therapon Hall?"

"I guess we are, Son. I don't even wanna see Derick—
that evil snake."

Alois was standing by her beliefs as she walked harder
and faster. No amount of money was worth letting people
film a death in her family, and for what? For ratings? For
gold-plated trophies at those fancy award shows—jacked
up on fruity pills and champagne, gossiping over what
designer duds everyone's been loaned? Then those show
people are driven to their mansions in road-hogging limos
so they can add their awards to their fireplace mantels and

vomit up enough money that could buy workin' folks a good used truck.

"Then what are we gonna do after we get Tara-Belle?" asked Presley.

Alois didn't know how to answer him. Her chest felt like a band of monkeys was jumping around inside. She nearly knocked down an elderly man who was waiting to cross the intersection she just passed.

"Maw, wait for me!" Presley shouted way behind her. A turning truck had trapped him on the sidewalk.

Alois tapped her foot, waiting, looking up stiff-necked at the clouds where her lord and traitor reclined on his solid-gold throne, getting foot massages by the angels. What the hell did she lack? How did her family become so bad off that they had lost their home and everything? She bet her neighbors back home were cackling with delight over her failure.

After Presley caught up to her, panting and wheezing, they passed more waste of good stones and bricks— palaces—selling things nobody needed really. Alois got a feeling she would die of malnutrition while scrubbing toilets for pennies—drown in one before the last flush of soapy ammonia. And what was worse: she couldn't blame her husband for his part in their homelessness, not now. Besides, what good would it do? Maybe I should end things faster and jump from the top of a ladder, Alois decided. She collapsed onto the concrete and buried her head in her hands, rocking, as tears rolled down her trembling arms.

"Of course Levi didn't kill himself—not knowingly—not in his right mind," cried Alois, while Presley tried to shield her from onlookers with his body. "How could I think such? Taylan messed with the ladder. He—"

"It's gonna be okay, Maw," said Presley in a sweet voice.

Alois thought back to her youth: Both Levi's and her parents never encouraged them to get an education or had any means to help them. The only thing Alois could guess was Levi's mother got tired of Millie and her sister judging everyone. From the tales Levi told about his Pentecostal preacher father, the man must've surely given them a dose of their judgmental crap big time. That would surely have caused those English snobs to disapprove of Levi's parents getting married.

A few yards farther down the road, a car honked behind them as they continued walking, only now Alois was limping slightly.

"That must be that son of a bitch Derick," huffed Alois, while the car kept "hooting," as the locals called it. "Keep walking and ignore 'im."

"But, Maw, it's not Derick. I think it's Mr. Gordon—the man with that production company who said we were human traffic."

The car pulled up beside Alois. Presley was right; it was Tom Gordon with Cinema Singular Productions. This was the last thing Alois wanted to see, another greedy reality-show producer.

"Leave us alone!" Alois hissed, giving him the finger

before picking up her pace down the sidewalk. She passed a sculpture-covered building for financial planning consultants and a sick chill traveled over her body. Someday her children would come to the same realization about their parents and blame her, Alois, for them not having anything. She couldn't let that happen whatever she did. She was going to have to encourage her children to get an education, no matter if them colleges were trying to turn kids into worldly heathens who believe folks evolved from apes. That was degrading, so Alois made Presley and Tara-Belle learn how God created man from mud and women from Adam's rib. And they weren't ever gonna forget it if she had anything to do with it.

"Mrs. Gurney, how marvelous. I see you managed to escape your abductors. Fancy a lift?" asked Tom Gordon, yelling out the car window. "I heard the awful news about Levi. I tried to warn you about old Millie and Derick. What they have done to your lovely family is unforgivable. I'm prepared to pay you two hundred thousand pounds if you let me interview you."

"*Humph*," Alois snorted and continued forward before pausing with a jolt. "Wait. How much did you say?" She grabbed Presley's arm and turned to face Tom.

"Do pardon me. I forget you are American—what with Derick and Suki altering your identities and all. I'm prepared to pay you over two hundred and seventy thousand U.S. dollars," said Tom, checking in the mirror for traffic.

"What's the catch?" asked Alois.

"I just need you to tell me your story—the true story of how Derick lured you here—your awful experiences in Therapon Hall. The world is right eager to know the real Gurney family. Think of how many people your survival story might help."

"You got a deal, fellah. But first, can ya take me to Therapon Hall? I need to fetch my daughter."

"It would be my pleasure, Mrs. Gurney—my pleasure indeed," said Tom. He jumped out of the car and opened the back door for Alois and Presley, who climbed inside. After a few turns, Tom handed Alois what looked like a large cellphone.

"Mrs. Gurney, I know this will be hard for you to watch, but it'll help you make sense of everything that has happened to your lovely family. Just press the triangle in the center of the pad."

Alois pressed the button, and horrific old scenes of Black slaves appeared on the screen, some with shackles on their hands and feet and scars covering their backs. Then the video showed modern images, including human trafficking victims of every race. Many of them were so deeply disturbing, they had dark squares covering parts of their bodies. Feeling feverish and queasy, Alois tossed the pad under the front seat before Presley could see any more of the graphic images of abducted adults and children. She had never seen pictures that awful in her childhood schoolbooks. In fact, she hardly remembered discussions about slavery at all. The narrator's voice soon stopped talking, and before she could ask Tom how that disgusting video was supposed to help her, they had reached the estate.

"I'll wait here in the car," said Tom. "I suggest you hurry, Mrs. Gurney. Trust me; you all will be in danger if Derick catches you trying to escape."

Alois tumbled out of the car and vomited before she and Presley ran inside to find Tara-Belle.

"She's in her room!" cried Alois. "Thank the heavens my precious baby is in her room."

"Where's Daddy?" Tara-Belle asked, playing with her doll, making it fold her socks on the bed.

"He's gone to Heaven, sweetie."

"When's he coming back, Mummy?"

"Soon, Tara," Alois lied, as she and Presley gathered their suitcases of belongings. It wasn't much, but Alois knew she would need her passport and other forms of identification. And she knew now wasn't the time to explain things to her daughter.

Ten minutes later, Tom grabbed their luggage and threw it in the trunk of his car. And after they all climbed inside, Egghead ran toward the car, barking. With everything that had happened, Alois had forgotten all about the dog.

"We can't leave Egghead," squealed Tara-Belle, before Presley opened his door for the dog to jump inside.

Derick, Suki, and Millie pulled up the gravel drive behind them. Derick leaned his head out the window. His face twisted with rage.

"Tom Gordon! What the hell are you doing? Are you

stealing my cast?" yelled Derick.

"Hang on to your knickers, Mrs. Gurney," said Tom. The car jerked as he sped toward the gate, flinging gravel like bullets.

Alois and Presley looked through the back window of the car. Derick was chasing after them, cutting through the ruined formal garden. In the back seat, Millie clasped her hands over her eyes. A sculpted boxwood hedge lodged itself in Derick's front fender like a spiraled animal horn ready to bore itself into Tom's bumper.

"Cool!" laughed Presley. "I've always wanted to race."

What had Alois gotten her family into? Would she and her kids soon meet Levi in the dreary overhead clouds? She still wasn't good with heights. Soon the two cars competed in a screeching match, and a path of tire smoke trailed them. Alois was getting dizzy from all the sharp turns, and Tom's shouts of victory nearly gave her a stroke.

"Ha! Serves him right!" he continued.

Alois looked back, and past a few toppled mailboxes, Derick's car had come to a stop and was now angled in a ditch, and Millie's rear end was sticking up over the edge of the back seat. Presley's giggles faded, and his face became frozen in terror. Tara-Belle crawled below the back seat while Egghead howled.

A half-hour later, Tom arrived at Old Blighty Towers in Fawsley. Two attendants in navy-blue suits took the Gurney family's luggage and opened the heavy wooden doors for them to enter the sprawling stone hotel. Alois was stunned at how grand everything was. The only hotel anywhere near where she was from had a flat roof and rooms lined up like a prison hall of cells—a sad sight except for the patches of peeling metal where apparent rust and graffiti had been painted over with mismatched shades of pea-soup green. And the only thing there you could even call a garden was a gravel-filled ring in the middle of the crumbling parking lot sporting an old wagon wheel and puny cactus with foam cups stuck to its thorns. Here at the Old Blighty Towers, the gardens were perfectly sculpted into a rambling work of art.

Inside the lobby, everything was so majestic and serene compared to the tumble they all went through to get there. Alois felt as though she looked like she had crawled straight out of a clothes dryer. Tom gave the doorman a handful of cash.

"I'll be needing the north tower sitting room now, please, Albert," he said. "Oh, and do make sure no one interrupts me until I'm finished interviewing."

"Of course, Sir," said the doorman. "Right this way." He escorted Tom, Alois, and her children through the hotel with a massive sunken garden in the middle under a stained-glass dome. The sound of a distant violin blended beautifully with the sprinkling water from a fountain of a naked woman as they passed on their way to the north tower. Presley tripped on a curved step because he kept his eyes on the fountain.

"Oooo, Mummy, Presley's lustin' at that woman's nekid boola," said Tara-Belle, pointing at the wet statue.

"Am not! She ain't real," groaned Presley, rubbing his

knee where he fell. "Nothin' here is real. When can we go home, Maw?"

"As soon as we can. Now y'all quit all this bellyaching," said Alois. She didn't know how to answer the question. She had no money to bury Levi, much less use a payphone.

They walked into the beige sitting room as the evening sun cast a golden glow over the white trim and real gold details. Tall, rounded windows surrounded the room except for the marble fireplace that was so huge, Alois could even see herself contently living inside it if all else failed. Egghead seemed to think the same thing as he plopped down on all fours near the cool stones.

Tom instructed Alois and her children to sit on the striped sofa under the crystal chandelier. He began setting up his video camera, which he unpacked from the luggage the attendants left on the rug half as big as a football field. He then adjusted the camera buttons and looked over the top of the camera.

"No. No. Your appearance won't do a'tall," said Tom.

"I'm sorry," said Alois, trying not to cry. She pushed a few loose strands of her hair back from her face before checking to see if her clothes were on right. "It's been a hard day for us all."

"No, what I mean is you all look too proper," said Tom. He messed up all their hair and ripped Presley's shirt. "The world wants to see the real Gurneys; they want to see how you were snatched from your normal American lives and forced into slave labor—exploited for profit on a fake reality show. The world wants to hear your real story. Do you understand, Mrs. Gurney?"

Alois nodded, feeling a bit less embarrassed.

"Good," said Tom. He took a check from his briefcase and filled it out before showing it to Alois. "Now, this is the money I promised you, and it is yours as soon as you all share your stories with the world."

"I'm sorry," said Alois. "You gotta give me and my kids a minute to relax. We're all stressed. That's—"

"That's the way the world expects you all to be," said Tom, pounding his fist into his hand with lifted eyebrows. "Give me that stress. Give me that brokenness and desperation. You all've been snatched from your homeland—forced into new identities against your will. You've been lied to, abused, attacked, aaand when you see the green light on the camera, I need you to give that to me."

Before Alois could respond, Tom switched on the green light and jumped in front of the camera.

"The whole world's been waiting with remote controls in hand, wondering whatever became of the Gurney family over the past week. The Benefactrix . . . seemingly plucked from the airwaves right after teams of international reporters and police descended on Therapon Hall during a historical re-enactment that went horribly awry: A mansion looted, secrets exposed, and all leading up to murder by dawn. Today I rescued the surviving family members who managed to escape from their cruel abductors. Found them wandering lost and confused through the streets of Northamptonshire, where they were soon pursued by their captors in a dangerous car chase that nearly ended with more death and destruction today. And all at the hands of Derick Hosier, a shady Hollywood producer who runs a human trafficking ring and further exploits and tracks his victims in bogus reality shows. And just who killed Levi Gurney? This is Tom Gordon, and welcome to my exclusive interview with the surviving members of the Gurney family." He handed Alois a box of tissues and eased into the chair in front of the sofa.

"Daddy's not killed. Daddy's in Heaven," said Tara-Belle. She snatched a tissue from the box and placed it on top of her head like a hat. Presley kept looking into the camera and lowering his droopy eyes.

"I know this has been a harrowing ordeal for you and your family, Mrs. Gurney. But before we discuss the events leading up to your husband's murder, the world would like to know the events that led to your abduction from your home in Wadebridge, Mississippi—a virtually unknown early settlement in the poorest and most infamous part of the United States still prided by locals today as the Deep South. Tell us, Mrs. Gurney, were you in your yard, hanging laundry out to dry when the abduction occurred? Or were you snatched from your beds in the middle of the night, like so many other victims?"

"No, no, it wasn't nothing like that. We weren't abducted," said Alois. She began to wonder if she had overlooked something from that day when Derick and

Suki arrived on their property in the limo.

"Understandable, Mrs. Gurney, understandable," said Tom gently. He leaned forward in his chair and grabbed her hand. "Confusion and denial are common reactions to trauma for many abductees, sometimes leading to Stockholm syndrome. Thinking back to that awful time, can you perhaps remember a point during your captivity where you and your family might have formed some sort of psychological bond with your captors?"

"I'm afraid I can't give you the answers you're looking for," said Alois. "But they did tell us we had to keep quiet about the plans and not tell a soul."

"That's one of the first steps in abduction case— silencing the victims," said Tom, sitting back proudly in his chair.

"Derick said we were supposed to get an inheritance from Levi's relative here in England. We were broke and needed the money," continued Alois, trying to remember the details as they happened.

"So that's when you fell for Derick's scheme, never knowing his plans to turn an innocent family, such as yourselves, into domestic servants—sold to the very woman you thought was a long-lost relative? At some point, do you remember your abductors making you repeat things you didn't want to say?"

"Well, just the English accents we had to practice over and over," said Alois with hesitation.

"The home viewers picked up on your accents," said Tom. "Many accused you of being phony, of trying to steal Lady Pimbledon's fortune when there was never any fortune there at all as was recently uncovered. But then— then there were viewers like me who suspected something much more sinister beneath the fake accents and phony titles forced upon you. After all, why would someone who was supposedly nearly royal be forced to wear a servants' uniform just one day after arriving as guests at Therapon Hall? Why would a lord and lady be put to work in dangerous situations which ultimately led to your husband's death?"

"Yes, we were doing as we were told," said Alois. "Truth is, we had it better at Therapon Hall than we ever did. We were hoping to get a little money for once, but even after we learned Millie was broke, well, we were too. What else could we do? We couldn't afford to return to Mississippi even if we tried to—especially when our home is gone."

"Ah, but why, Mrs. Gurney? What did Derick tell you?"

"We were told our home was bulldozed down," said Alois, with a pit of shame and confusion gnawing at her stomach.

"I know this might be difficult to hear, Mrs. Gurney, but sometimes captives are drugged and brainwashed," said Tom, pushing back in his chair and placing two fingers under his chin.

Something or someone banged against the door outside the sitting room. The door opened, and the doorman fell across the floor and hit his head against the leg of a marble table. Derick, Suki, and Millie stepped over his body and rushed to the center of the room.

"Tom Gordon! I knew it. Still trying to ruin me with your lies," growled Derick. He swatted the camera off the tripod, and it smashed against the rug.

"How dare you try to destroy the evidence!" hissed Tom, bounding from his chair as the doorman stood to his feet. "I demand you get these thugs out of this hotel."

"I do apologize, Sir. But they forced their way inside. I'll go and get the owner," said the doorman.

"You mean Charles Whitmire?" asked Millie. She straightened her pillbox hat, which had shifted to the side of her messed-up hair.

"That would be the owner, yes," said the doorman, adjusting his crumpled suit. "And rest assured, Mr. Whitmire doesn't deal too kindly with hooligans."

"I'm certain Charlie will simply be delighted to see me. My ancestors helped fund this hotel," said Millie, with her eyebrows lifted. "He named a luxury suite here in my name, in fact. Of course, I insisted he do no such thing."

"You don't mean—you are THE Lady Pimbledon?" choked the doorman. "I do beg your pardon." The doorman bowed and began to ease backward out of the sitting room. "Here, let me get you a bottle of our finest wine and some caviar while we prepare your suite."

"That won't be necessary," said Millie.

"It's the least I could do, Your Ladyship. It's such an honor to have you—such an honor."

"Evidence? What evidence?" Derick asked Tom after

the doorman left.

"You see, Mrs. Gurney here was just confessing to being a victim to your human trafficking ring—a ring you operate under the guise of a legitimate reality show," said Tom.

Derick's arms rose and dropped in frustration. "Oh now, Mrs. Gurney, you surely don't believe this idiot—this, this nonsense that we abducted your family."

"Nonsense?" sneered Tom, crossing his arms. "As it so happens, I have a full confession from another victim of yours—a woman by the name of Ms. Johns."

"Lady Pimbledon's maid?" asked Derick. "That's preposterous."

Tom took three bold steps toward Derick. "She claims you sold her to Millie. The poor woman had to go into hiding to keep you from finding her."

"What? I did no such thing." Millie staggered in place with her fingers tugging her pearl necklace. "I have never purchased anyone. Why, when Ms. Johns came to work for me, she didn't even have a car or a roof over her head."

"I'm sorry, Tom," sighed Alois. "I'm sorry I can't go along with this—this setup. Ms. Johns is a two-timing bitch. She ain't hiding from Derick and Suki. She's hiding from the cops because she helped steal half of Millie's stuff—she and the other servants. Saw it with my own eyes." Alois held two trembling fingers in front of her grimacing face.

"Oh, thank you, dear woman," said Millie. Her chest heaved, and she collapsed onto the padded arm of the nearest available chair. "The press accused me of selling my furniture to pay off my debts. My insurance company accused me of destroying my own property to collect on insurance. I've been called a lying drunkard, a murderer, and now I'm being accused of human trafficking. My upstanding reputation has been ruined."

Tom knelt in front of Alois and patted her hand again. "Mrs. Gurney, you are making a terrible mistake. You are suffering from Stockholm syndrome." Tom flashed the check he had earlier written. "This money can change your life. I will personally see to it that you and your family get the best professional counseling."

Alois removed her hand, and Tom sprang upright with a jagged smile. "Have you received any payment from Derick, Mrs. Gurney?"

"No," said Alois. Now that she thought about it, she never recalled them discussing getting money from Derick for starring in the reality show. The only money she was told she would get was an inheritance from Millie.

"Don't you see, Mrs. Gurney? Those people standing over there haven't paid you a single pence for all your back-breaking work, and now they have murdered your husband," said Tom, pointing to Millie, Derick, and Suki.

Millie placed a trembling hand to her forehead. Her chin quivered. "Go ahead . . . finish me off. Sue me for anything I have left. But I swear I didn't kill Levi. I should have believed you, Mrs. Gurney. You tried to warn me that the servants were trying to harm your family."

"I, uh, have something I need to get off my chest," said

Alois. She couldn't stand to see Millie suffer. "We're not victims of human trafficking. Now, I ain't sayin' one of the servants didn't do something to Levi's ladder. My husband was terminally ill. I'm surprised he made it as long as he did." Alois broke into sobs, and Presley and Tara-Belle scooted as close as they could against her in one big hug. She wiped her tears with her free hand. "Levi fought with everything in him to be on the reality show—to try and provide for his family before he—before he went to Heaven. When he heard Millie had no inheritance to give, I think he climbed that ladder on purpose. I don't think he wanted to die laid up in no bed, gasping for his last breath, realizing he had failed me and the kids." Alois breathed out hard. She had been holding this bitter secret for too long.

"I have a confession, as well, Mrs. Gurney," said Millie, waddling up to Alois like a beaten puppy. "I was lonely and afraid. My social circles dropped me before you all came here. I wanted someone to take care of me in my old age, so I lied about having liver disease. I led the other servants to believe they'd receive a substantial inheritance if they could just hold out until I died. When Derick made me an offer to film the reality show, I couldn't pass up the money. I suppose he will be suing me, too."

"I'm not gonna sue you, Millie," said Alois. "But you ain't as bad off as you think. You don't really know what poor is."

"Oh, dear woman. I'm afraid I misjudged you. What a wonderfully unique family you have. If there's anything I

178

can do to make up for my poor treatment of you. I might not be able to do as much as I would like, of course," said Millie.

Alois positioned her children on both sides of her and lowered her head. "We don't belong here. All I want is to get back home and bury my husband in the red clay he grew up playing in."

Tom fumbled about, picking up the pieces of his camera off the floor before he stormed out of the sitting room. Derick Hosier remained with a determined expression.

"But, Lady Pimbledon! Mrs. Gurney! You can't quit the show . . . not now. We can still make some kind of go at this. I mean, hit reality shows aren't really reality anyway," Derick laughed nervously.

Suki put her fists on her hips. "Derick, you can fire me if you want to, but the ratings have plummeted, and you know it. The Benefactrix has already been canceled in several countries. People are right angry with the way the Gurney family was treated. It's time to cut our losses; call it even."

Derrick paced back and forth with his lips and fists clenched.

"All right then," he said. "Consider your job position cut as well, Suki." He mumbled and huffed all the way out of the room.

Alois flashed Suki a look of sympathy. "I just don't understand. You mean, you left England to work for that jerk?"

"Derick hired me as an assistant, but he thinks of me more as his secretary. I left London after struggling to get any real work in film production. And though there is much more of an industry here, breaking through the celluloid ceiling is tough enough if you are a woman, but try living in my designer shoes." Suki smiled knowingly and lifted her leg, exposing her chunky heels.

"Those are some fierce shoes, as they say." Alois tried to appear nonjudgmental for a change.

"You wear my shoes, Mrs. Gurney, and you'll start looking past people's surfaces, even past your own comfort, and you start finding potential. Too many people surrender to hopelessness because they don't have the influence to know where to begin. If you aren't born into privilege or know the right people, you just have to keep striving to make good connections, learn all you can, until you have that influence."

"Derick will calm down in a day or two," continued Suki. "On another subject, I have something I believe you might want to see, Alois." Suki opened her pink leather briefcase, removed a fat gold envelope, and handed it to Alois.

"What is this—legal papers against me?" asked Alois.

"No," laughed Suki. "Those are donations from your fans. It should be enough to get you back home and cover expenses."

Alois removed her arm from around her children. "You mean I have fans?"

"Yes. Especially online."

"You mean on the Mason-Dixon line?" asked Alois, still in shock.

"No, on the internet and social media." Suki patted the envelope. "Mrs. Gurney, I believe you will find that you and your family have made a jammy impression on people. That envelope came from the president of your fan club, plus I included my share of the show's royalties. I know how much your children need it. Do not let them quit school."

Presley peeled away from his mother and gave Suki a hug.

Alois felt a conflicting flood of shame wash over her for the first time. "I'm afraid I don't deserve this, but you are right; my kids do. I'm embarrassed to say I lived my whole life under a delusion that I was, you know, better than some people."

"Better than people with my skin color, you mean?" said Suki, raising her eyebrows and angling her head forward with a weary smile.

"Yes," said Alois, feeling her face sweating worse than a whore in church, as they say. But that was the problem, she realized; she had swallowed everything her community had said, along with their hateful conspiracy beliefs.

She reached out and grabbed Suki's hand and struggled to keep a tear from spilling down her cheek. "As hard as it is to believe, being *White* made me feel like somebody; it was all I had, really. The best thing that ever happened to me was getting out of that small town and seein' how stupid it is to judge other people over their appearance or class. This whole experience has forced me to think about slavery—true slavery I can't even imagine."

Presley let go of Suki and hugged his mother. Suki waved her finger for Alois to stop speaking. She then placed her free hand over Alois's hand, and her smile was full now.

"Well, Mrs. Gurney, I think you have inherited the biggest gift of all."

CHAPTER FOURTEEN

Alois finished vacuuming the beige carpet in her new apartment. She pried her shoes from her aching feet and put them and her university staff ID badge on the closet shelf. She sat on the sofa and propped her feet on the coffee table while looking over her scheduled speaking engagements at the local women's university, where she was also working as a secretary in the office. Alois reflected over her life: Her home, seventy miles north in Wadebridge, Mississippi, had been swiped off the face of the Earth. The whole region had snubbed her and her children when they had returned to bury Levi in the local cemetery. She had changed her hair, wardrobe, and attitude, but nothing could have prepared her for the backlash in her change of speech. She had no idea how hostile people would react because someone's accent had changed. You would have thought her family had betrayed the entire world to the extra-terrestrials. People somehow feel threatened when you try that hard to better yourself, Alois realized.

As far as public hostility, Alois was glad a judge had thrown out the lawsuit against Suki and Derick and had declared them not guilty of human trafficking and a list of other charges. In exchange for Alois agreeing to defend Derick and Suki, Derick decided to drop any lawsuits against the surviving Gurney family and Millie Pimbledon. Alois also insisted that Derick make Suki an equal partner in the production company.

Alois placed the schedule on the sofa and laughed. After her last speech in the university auditorium about how the reality show had changed her life, a fan had approached Alois, among the thousands of young women, to tell her the latest news. It seems Wadebridge, Mississippi, regretted bulldozing down her house after all. Fans from across the globe had been traveling there, hoping to see the now vacant spot of overgrown weeds where her home once stood. The city erected a plaque, marking the Gurney family's property, but they regretted the loss of profits they could've had from charging for home tours.

Egghead, the hound, lay at the end of the sofa, groaning. The poor dog had been depressed ever since they came back to the United States. Alois assumed Egghead either missed Levi or hated being cooped up in a small apartment with no yard to run around on all day. The doorbell rang just as Alois reached for the remote control to the television.

"Don't tell me you lost your key again," yelled Alois, imagining it was Presley who was tired from hanging out with the neighborhood girls again. He liked to brag to the girls that Hollywood wanted him to audition for a television series. Unfortunately, that's all he could do is brag. Alois was the family provider now, and they couldn't afford to move to California.

Alois unlocked the door and blinked her eyes to see if she was hallucinating. It was a woman she hadn't seen in over three months—a woman not wearing a fancy dress but, instead, was wearing faded jeans, sandals, and a paisley-printed blouse with fringe sleeves.

"Lady Pimbledon!"

"It's just Millie now."

"You came here all the way from England? How did you find me?"

"Oh, it wasn't hard, dear," said Millie. "I saw you on the news, doing motivational speaking here. I've made a lot of changes as well, in fact. I quit drinking, settled my debts, and realized the importance of being myself."

"Please come inside," said Alois, stepping aside in the doorway. For once, she wasn't embarrassed for visitors to see her home.

"I can't stay, dear," said Millie, with a peculiar grin. She reached into a drawstring pouch draped across her shoulder and removed a piece of pale-blue paper. "I want you to have this. It's a check for my share of the reality show's profits and the sale of my estate."

In a dramatic sweep, Millie held the check tautly by the outer edges and placed it in the center of Alois's hand.

Alois eyed the long series of numbers on the check—numbers she had never written out even in her high school math class she could vaguely remember.

"But this is—for over three million dollars," choked

Alois. "You need this, Millie. I thought you were broke."

"I am—well, according to my ex-friends who think I'm destitute now that I'm down to two accountants!" giggled Millie, while in the parking lot, a scraggly man climbed out of an old van, which had been spray-painted with peace signs and flowers.

"It's rather liberating when the only thing one has to prove is that one has nothing left to prove. It's quite exhausting trying to impress a bunch of old snoots. Life's too short, and my new boyfriend adores me just the way I am," said Millie. The man danced up behind Millie and gave her a bear hug while a jagged-toothed grin spread over his unshaven chin. Alois found herself scratching her forehead in bewilderment.

"This here is my little sassy muffin," said the man. "Ain't she purty?"

Stunned air became trapped in Alois's lungs, sustaining her until she got her breathing pattern back. She nodded and remembered when she and Levi were young and the playful moods that often overtook him, especially when he was tipsy. And to think, several months ago, she believed Millie was near death. But why would she give Alois all her money? Millie did assure her she was sober.

"I thought it was time to get out of the house and really buckle down. I've always wanted to travel the United States in a van," giggled Millie. She tugged on a funky earring hanging down to her collar. "It's costume. Never worn it before."

Millie paused as if collecting her thoughts. "Again, I

want to apologize about Levi dying from that awful fall on the ladder. The police completed their investigation last night, and it turns out that Taylan Chowdhury was innocent. Oh, sure, Taylan got angry and destroyed my garden he worked so hard on, but that boy wouldn't gone that far."

"Who sawed through the ladder then?" asked Alois, still doubtful at this discovery.

"Why, it was the butler, Mr. Shaw, only as it turns out that wasn't his real name." Millie clasped her hand on Alois's crossed arms. "The scoundrel was after my fortune all this time. Oh, to think of the danger to which I subjected everyone. I'm such a fool."

"I'm not sure I understand," said Alois.

"My! Have you not been watching the news today, dear? All this time, Mr. Shaw was actually Lord Charles— a man I tried to get Levi's mother to marry years earlier. You see, after my niece, Mary, married Levi's father instead, Lord Charles's estate burned to the ground, and he lost everything. He ended up murdering a man by the name of Lord Richardson in a failed robbery attempt, and then he went into hiding. Years later, under the name Mr. Shaw, Charles sought employment at Therapon Hall. I never even recognized him. Charles confessed to the police that he wanted your whole family dead so he could inherit my estate. And if you ask me, I think Charles was jealous that Levi wasn't his son."

Alois realized that it must have been Mr. Shaw or Charles who tried to run her off the road back in

Northampton.

Egghead barked behind Alois and dashed out of the apartment, squeezing between her legs and the doorframe, while Tara-Belle gave chase.

"Egg, come back here!" Alois yelled, but the dog ran up to the back of the van and scratched the bumper with its paws.

"Aw, Sir Eggart must sense his sweet thing," giggled Millie.

"His sweet thing?" asked Alois, rushing toward the back of the van with Tara-Belle and the others.

The man opened the door to the trunk, and Alois saw Millie's poodle reclining in a basket beside three puppies that looked half like her hound, Egghead. One had black and white spots, and the other two were blonde and white. Egg and the poodle barked joyfully at one another and licked each other's noses. Egghead jumped in the trunk and laid on the other side of the puppies, inspecting them while his tail drummed against the van floor.

Presley came riding up on his bicycle and spotted Millie and the dogs.

"Oh wow! Egghead had puppies?"

"Boy dogs can't have puppies, dummy," Tara-Belle sassed Presley.

"I know that, but he's the father." Presley reached into the van and stroked the puppies.

"Come on, Egghead. Millie's gotta leave, and you can't go with her," said Alois, slapping her knees playfully.

Egghead barked, moved behind Millie's poodle, and

placed one paw on his puppies.

"Oh, dear. It looks like you'll have to keep the whole lot of them," said Millie. "We can't separate a happy family."

Presley looked at the dogs and his forehead wrinkled with worry. "But, Maw, what're we gonna do? The apartment manager won't let us have more than one dog."

Alois held up the check Millie had given her. "Well then, we'll have to buy us a house in California with a big yard, won't we?"

With grins as big as Texas, Presley and Tara-Belle scooped up the puppies and baby-talked them.

Alois's eyes became misty. She wished to everything that Levi was with her to see his family's change in fortune—to not have to speed dry their underwear over a flaming barrel. She would still let him call her Smokie, though.

The End

ABOUT THE AUTHOR

Multi-Award-Winning Author Milan Sergent studied creative writing in college and began writing the novel series "Candlewicke 13" in 2007, a year after featuring some of the series' characters in his solo art exhibition, titled "Outsiders and Apparitions," near Rockefeller Center in New York City.

An artist and poet since adolescence, a few of Sergent's early poetic works were published in Scarlet Literary Magazine and more recently in his two illustrated poetry books, "Outsiders and Apparitions: Possessed Poems and Art for Family Picnics" and "Martyrs and Manifestations: Hexed Poems and Art for Holiday Gatherings." He lives with his wife of 30 years, Beatrice H. Crew, who is also an award-winning author.

To learn more about the author or his works, visit www.milansergent.com. While there, join the mailing list for important news updates and notifications about future novel releases.

ALSO AVAILABLE BY MILAN SERGENT

Outsiders and Apparitions

The Pitrick family picnic went off without a hitch until Patty drove the unwelcome wagon into a roadside ditch. Her daughter cried out with maddening dread while apparitions appeared high overhead. She didn't take it as a sign that Patty was dead, but that the crash had mashed her sauerkraut sandwich.

Outsiders and Apparitions: Possessed Poems and Art for Family Picnics by Milan Sergent is an eclectic book of poetry and art by an easily bored author and artist who broke free from gross boundary violations, conformity demands, and abandonment as a youth. The past now only apparitions: he is currently possessed with a mission to encourage expression without dull traditions, rules, or shackling expectations. The soul can be possessed, but the product it produces must be free to protest.

Praise for *Outsiders and Apparitions*
Possessed Poems and Art for Family Picnics

"This superb collection of poetry and art, Outsiders and Apparitions by Milan Sergent, cleverly confronts societal opinions on outward success, happiness, and inner fulfillment. . . . Each poem is illustrated with the most extraordinary and exceptional artwork. I was absolutely captivated by this collection. Milan is such an inspirational artist and writer. His talent for provoking thought and change in human behavior is superb. . . ."

—Lesley Jones for *Readers' Favorite*

"This is the best book of poetry that I have read this year. I absolutely enjoyed the ingenious poetry that Sergent brought to life in this collection. . . . What I loved even more was the collection of paintings that accompanied each poem. . . . Overall, I think Milan Sergent has created a masterpiece. . . . It's definitely a collection I would recommend. I can't wait to read more of his work."

—Tiffany Ferrell for *Readers' Favorite*

"[A] fabulous combination of art and poems that are unique, fresh, and unconventional and take readers to another realm altogether. . . . The collection is eclectic, unapologetic, and fantastical, and is a good way to make readers break free from their traditional ways of expressing themselves and to try out something different."

—Mamta Madhavan for *Readers' Favorite*

"Sergent brings a unique brand of surrealism to an emotionally resonant space in this collection, which explores personal and wider themes that play with structure and form in poetry, but also express a breakout from the conventions of language, art, and society. . . . Having been an ardent fan of Milan Sergent's fiction work for quite some time now, it was a delight to explore another facet of the author's mind and see his artistic process come to light in new forms. . . . Outsiders and Apparitions is a book that no poetry fan should be without."

—K.C. Finn for *Readers' Favorite*

"Milan Sergent's Outsiders and Apparitions is a collection of poetry and artwork that has a way of digging into almost all of your senses. His poetry has a lyrical, children's nursery rhyme sort of bent, but with an adult flavor and tone. An antiquated essence also paints every page, so that there is a feeling of transportation that takes us centuries back into the past."

—Erin Nicole Cochran for *Readers' Favorite*

Martyrs and Manifestations

This is an eclectic book of poetry and art by an easily bored author and artist who broke free from gross boundary violations, conformity demands, and abandonment in his youth.

With oppressive forces still clawing from the grave, and people who try to shame or silence victims and embarrassing history, Sergent is currently on a mission to encourage expression without dull traditions, rules, or shackling expectations. Authoritarians can leave us feeling hexed, but you can break the spell.

Praise for Martyrs and Manifestations
Hexed Poems and Art for Holiday Gatherings

"As a fan of Milan Sergent in general, I anticipated getting into another excellent collection of verses and art, and I was once again thoroughly impressed. . . . There is a really quirky mix of traditionalism and celebration of the poetic form which Sergent cleverly subverts and twists into new rule-breaking permutations to delight and surprise his readers. . . . The underlying themes, empathy, and emotional quality of the work are second to none, clearly coming from a real place within the author which we marginalized folk can all relate to. Overall, I would highly recommend Martyrs and Manifestations . . . to poetry fans, surrealists, and the oppressed seeking freedom the world over."
—K.C. Finn for *Readers' Favorite*

"Martyrs and Manifestations is indeed a masterpiece and I would recommend it to all poetry lovers to read and appreciate the poet's aesthetic abilities, imagination, and creative mind. It is one of the best poetry collections I have come across in recent times . . . ."
—Mamta Madhavan for *Readers' Favorite*

"Engaging storytelling . . . bursts with odd, witty, playful incidents and characters. The narrative continually surprises . . . charming . . . laugh-out-loud funny."

— The BookLife Prize by *Publishers Weekly*
for Book Two of the Candlewicke 13 Series.

"Whether you're a younger reader or just young at heart, this is a very immersive, high-quality fantasy series that never ceases to amaze me with its imaginative quality and new twists to the plot."

— K.C. Finn for *Readers' Favorite*

"Vibrant and funny . . . ."   — The Booklife Prize by *Publishers Weekly*
for Book One of the Candlewicke 13 Series.